APR 3 0 2015

Ridgway Library District

S0-CBP-413

APR 3 0 2015

# SALVATION

## OF A

# SERIAL

# CELIBATE

*A True Story*

GREGORY McALLISTER

Copyright © 2014 Greg McAllister. All rights reserved.

This book includes a thorough revision and re-write of *Confessions of a Serial Celibate: Book One: The Joyful Mysteries* (self-published, 225 pp, 2003).

No part of this book may be reproduced, stored in a retrieval system, or transmitted by any means, electronic, mechanical, photocopying, recording, or otherwise, without written permission from the author.

www.gregorymcallister.com

For Élan and Shane

# ACKNOWLEDGMENTS

I am especially grateful to five people: my friend Arthur Westing for his encouragement and proofreading; my editor, Suzanne Kingsbury, who taught me how to see through my pen; Jaimie Johnson for her cover photography; my son, Shane McAllister who formatted the book and designed the cover; and my partner, Linda Evans, who daily inspires me with her love and positive energy.

Thanks to my many seminary friends and classmates who shared my youthful idealism and adolescent cynicism. Thanks also to my former wives who had to put up with my arrested development. The names of the latter have been changed to protect the intimate.

# PROLOGUE

## THE MANICHAEAN CANDIDATE

In the backyard, a basketball hoop stands between the fig trees along the wire fence. My dad has strung chicken wire between the fence and the slatted backboard to keep the ball from going into the Peck's yard. Jim Boy and Tony stand beneath it, beckoning me down for a game. I leave my Grandma Mayme with her sensible black shoes and tortoise shell combs and run out for a pick-up game, dribbling around rotting figs and fermenting apples, sweat rolling down my back until my hair is matted and my shirt cast off.

After Jim Boy and Tony are called home, I head for the kitchen to get a drink, and poke my head into my grandma's room on the way. It's a hot muggy June day. The air is heavy with the smell of the Ben Gay I have tirelessly massaged into her shoulders. She sits stone-like in her rocking chair, rosary beads wrapped around her pudgy fingers, her eyes shut. She is whispering prayers. A partly-crocheted rug lies at her feet. On the wall beside her, Jesus kneels against a jagged rock, blood and sweat oozing from his temples, an angel hovering behind him. "Hi, Gramma," I say quietly.

She opens her eyes briefly, then creases her forehead and turns toward the wall, showing me her tight perfect bun.

My stomach grabs. "What's the matter, Gramma?"

She keeps her face to the wall, her hands moving on the rosary. "I'm surprised, that's all," she says.

I try to still my breath. The sweat runs in rivulets down my back. My eyes sting.

"And I'm disappointed," she says. Her tone is the one she uses to talk about sinners, lax Catholics. "I didn't think you were that weak."

"What do you mean?" I whisper. Hot tears run down my cheeks.

My grandmother turns her fierce face to me. "You couldn't keep that shirt on?" she narrows her eyes "and offer your suffering up for the poor souls in Purgatory?"

Like a heroic Gawain donning armor, I pull my shirt back on. My grandmother continues looking on in disapproval, cinching me into her delicately stitched, but inflexible, religious corset, judging me along with the other laggards, putting moral stricture over love, dividing good and evil along the dotted line first drawn by Zoroaster in 600 BC when God had two sons and the first chose Good and Truth, the other, Evil and Falsehood.

Eight centuries later, a Persian named Mani would introduce this dualism into Christianity by teaching that the human body was a dark prison confining the light of man's soul, that only a strict, almost violent, asceticism could free the soul from its fleshy prison. The doctrine would morph its way down through Augustine and the medieval Jansenists, and by the time my Grandmother learned it from the Benedictine nuns and then passed it down to me, it would be the basic operating system in the Catholic computer.

I am seven the summer the Second World War ends and my grandparents come from Montana to live with us. My father adds a room to our little house in Kentfield he and my mother bought for $3000 when they were first married. That was just after the Golden Gate Bridge was built, and rather than taking the ferry, my father drives across it to work at the base of Market Street in a dusty three-man trucking office wedged between noisy loading docks. I ride the bus every day to St. Anslem's grammar school, a three sided mission-style building with stucco walls and a long arcade lined with low green benches where we salute the cross and the flag and then wait for the sound of the wooden clacker so we can run out to the cement playground. Nuns watch from the sidelines in their black crepe robes, their faces framed with starched white linen.

German, Irish and Italian, the kids of St. Anslem's are all Catholic, and the Catholics are under siege. We know this because the nuns make us pray for Cardinal Mindszenty, who is being tortured in a Hungarian prison. They make us pray for the overthrow of the Communists, including Jews, Protestants, Masons, and the owner of Jack's Drug Store, who sells girlie magazines.

Every day I wear a uniform with salt and pepper cord pants to a school that smells of crayons, floor wax, baloney and ripe bananas from the lunchboxes in the cloakroom. One afternoon, I grab my lunch pail from the cloakroom and run out the door, banging into something on the arcade, something dark and scratchy, and I can't get loose. Things are bouncing off my head, hands grab me, spinning me around, pushing me out into the light. Finally, I look up and see a giant, red-faced nun, shaking her finger, telling me not to run in the corridor. I realize I was lost in the black crepe folds of her habit, tangled in her rosary beads, dangling scissors, and wooden clacker, trapped there like a flightless bird.

I end up not liking nuns much. In third grade I call Sister Mary Coleman an old goat under my breath, and she grabs my arm, shakes it, yanks me toward the door and down the empty arcade toward the boys' bathroom, where she stiff-arms the old green door, and drags me to the wash trough with its spring-loaded faucets and the soap dispensers you have to jiggle on the bottom to get the Boraxo out. She jiggles out a handful of powder. "Open, boy!"

I open my mouth and she slaps the powder into it, then cups her hand under the faucet.

"Open!" Her hand splats over my mouth. Water softens the coarse powder. "Now chew, boy!"

I hate her. I want to spit it in her face, run out of there, but I remember Grandma at home, and what she has taught me about suffering. I start chewing, offering the pain up for the "poor souls." I know, at that moment, God loves me more than He loves Sister Mary Coleman.

I never tell anyone at home when I get into trouble because they'd side with the nuns. Instead I tell it in confession on Saturday. "Bless me, Father, it's been one week since my last confession. I used swear words five times, disobeyed my mom twice, and called Sister Mary Coleman an old goat." I always have little sins to confess, cussing, getting angry, fighting, never the big ones Grandma talks about – missing Mass on Sunday, eating meat on Friday. And definitely never *sins of the flesh*. I'm not even sure what those are. All I can imagine is blubber jiggling.

It's hot in the confessional. I rattle off my sins and wait. Father Leonard doesn't say anything. Then he clears his throat. I can see his mouth working close to the screen. "Uh, Greg, do you ever, when you're in bed, ever rub your penis?"

Wow! How does he know about that? I only recently learned how to do that. I thought it was my own discovery. When I say yes, he asks me if it feels good.

"Yes, Father," I say, "it feels really good."

He lets out a sigh. "What you're doing is very dangerous. It's called masturbation, and it's a mortal sin. If you don't stop right now you could end up in Hell. For your penance say three Our Fathers and three Hail Marys. And, uh, Greg, do you suppose you could cover the 8:30 Mass tomorrow?"

I'm Father's first-string altar boy. I started out as a torchbearer in the second grade. People told my mother that I looked like an angel on the altar. I wore a cassock and surplice and carried a big candle and had to kneel for a long time without getting sick from the incense. Grandma said even the pope probably started out as a torchbearer.

We're good Catholics. We say grace before meals, night prayers before bed, and after dinner we pray together with the radio. "It's almost time," my mother says, clearing the table. She puts the dishes in the sink and I twist the volume switch on the radio until I hear the sharp snap followed by the hum of tubes heating up. My father and grandfather kneel down. Grandma stays in her chair because of her arthritis, and I slump on the worn wicker chair, my forehead pressed into the woven backing. "This is The Rosary Hour with Father Alvin Wagner," the announcer says.

Weekends, we buy cokes and comics at Caesar's Soda Fountain, get our hair buzzed at Eldon's barber shop, hunt for nuts and bolts at Mueller's Hardware. On the way home we stop at Berthenier's station and use our gas ration stamps to fill up the brand new Chevy we've won at the St. Anselm's festival.

Tony Giusti and Jim-Boy Pulskamp are my best friends. We play at the little sandbar near the bridge, catching polliwogs in Folgers Coffee cans and use those same cans to pick blackberries, selling them for 25 cents a can. We make arrows from prickly-topped swamp weeds and attack the Hinkley gang up the hill throwing acorns and using garbage can lids as shields. I try to escape the stigma of being an only child and the void of lonely hours when my friends are home with their siblings by cultivating companions, co-conspirators.

I don't remember the exact moment I become Grandma Mayme's confidante. I know only the familiarity of her full round face, her stocky frame, the warmth of those hours spent in her room at her knee, shuffling her playing cards, which smell like camphor ice. She reads me tea leaves, gives me pennies and candy, bakes me cookies and blackberry pie. We play whist and rummy and Parcheesi. She shows me the holy cards she keeps in an old candy box, the ones the nuns gave her when she was a girl at St. Benedict's Academy. The cards have doily edges and show Jesus crucified, his heart stabbed with thorns, blood oozing out. The cards have different numbers on them. The plenary indulgence card, with no number, forgives everything. "If you recited this prayer and fell over dead," she says, "you'd go right to Heaven." In her silky flowery dresses, her crocheted afghan over her shoulders, she teaches me the magic of indulgences, saints' days, feast days, first Fridays, novenas. Rubbing Ben-Gay into her shoulders for her acute arthritis, I hear about the sins of the flesh, the redemptive power of the rosary, how self-denial strengthens the soul of a spiritual warrior. "Stick out your tongue," she says. "If you're fibbing, there will be a black mark down the middle." Sure enough, I find an ugly black line running down the length of my tongue whenever I lie. She tells me about St. Francis, a rich kid who gave away all his fancy clothes and money and dedicated his life to God and the birds. "Greggie," she says, "I don't care if you never make a cent. Just be a saint."

As new people move into the neighborhood, she ranks them on the scorecard of salvation, reserving her harshest judgments for those whose names indicate they should be Catholics, but aren't practicing. Even my parents do not escape. They enjoy an evening highball and are therefore weak. Tony's family goes to the 10:30 Mass. Mayme says that makes them not quite as good Catholics as us, because they're lazy. I find it exhilarating, pigeonholing people into simplistic categories. My grandmother stands at her bedroom window, watching Liz Peck whistle happily in her tomato patch. Turning to me with the offended look of a medieval inquisitor, she shakes her head slowly, pronouncing her anathema: *A whistling woman / and a crowing hen / bring the old devil / right out of his den*. My stomach sinks. I like Liz, but she's doomed to Hell.

When her arthritis gets really bad, Mayme offers it up, and I imagine streams of poor souls floating up to Heaven on contrails of Ben-Gay.

I watch my grandfather turn our back yard into an Eden of vegetables. His pleated pants are held up by worn suspenders, and he wears a stained, soft-brimmed hat cocked at an angle. His pipe is clamped between loose dentures, and his shirt is rolled to his elbows. Unlike my grandmother, Peter Kennedy is thin and wiry with high cheekbones that give him the appearance of the Native American Sioux he spent so much time with in North Dakota.

My grandmother's arthritis keeps her from the basement steps, and when the sun goes down, my grandfather will retreat to his basement lair, where he keeps his gardening tools and his stash of outlawed smoking materials hidden in an old Folgers can. Under the steps, he keeps a record of the first rainfall of each year, the first frost, the date of each year's spring planting. He grew up in the rolling green farmlands of Wabasha township on the Mississippi River, sixty miles south of St. Paul where Irish immigrants farmed land that resembled their native Ireland. As a boy, he delivered groceries in a horse-drawn wagon, and was instructed by his employer to hand his cargo over without resistance to the brash young Indians who frequently waylaid his wagon. He was the first person the local Sioux saw with fillings in his teeth, earning him the nickname "Hiamuga" or Iron Tooth. Later, he owned a trading post in North Dakota, learned to speak Sioux, went to pow-wows, learned their dances, caught tarantulas found in banana bunches delivered to the post and put them on display for his Sioux customers who were mesmerized by these strange prehistoric insects.

I will spend my childhood under the spell of my grandmother's Catholicism, lost in the black habit and rosary of that Manichean destiny. What I will discover when I finally emerge is that my grandfather's resonance with the pagan roots of our native Irish Catholicism, and his sensuous bond to the Earthly Mother is stronger than a beaded rosary, stronger than thorns and crosses, stronger than kneeling in a cassock for hours on end and praying to the radio, stronger even than that plenary indulgence card that is supposed to send me right to Heaven.

PART ONE:

# THE
# JOYFUL
# MYSTERIES

# 01

## FAT WIMP

When is our fate decided? When do the dominoes that eventually form the patterns of our lives begin to fall? Perhaps for me it began with St. Augustine, my grandmother's Manichean tendencies, St. Anselm's and the Catholic neighborhood that raised me. Or perhaps it started with the strange labyrinth of puberty.

1954: Eighth grade. The year of pegger pants, black wing tip shoes with horseshoe tap heels and white painted welts, the year of the duck's ass hairstyle with fishhooks dangling over the forehead. The official colors are pink and charcoal. You have to wear your MacGregor windbreaker with the collar up. Belts are skinny, pink suede and black-edged. The *'chuke* look. At first only Bocabella and the class hoods dress this way, but then Scabby, our substitute eighth grade teacher, snatched prematurely from a skin cancer operation, outlaws it, and the rest of us taste the forbidden fruit. I start timidly with the suede belt, then convince my mother I need a charcoal windbreaker. Next thing I know, I'm crashing out of the Junior Bootery in my first pair of horseshoe taps. The sound of that rebellious metal in the St. Anselm's arcade gives me the same unfamiliar sexual rush I got when I lit illicit fires down by the creek with matches filched from my grandfather's smoking can.

It's the year I beg God to make my grandmother better, the year I pray for her to come home from the hospital, but she doesn't. I plead with the poor souls to help, but she dies inside an oxygen tent without saying goodbye to me. It's also the year my grandfather begins to bloom. He laughs more, shows us Sioux dance steps, drinks an occasional glass of wine with my mother. In school I surprise myself and everyone else by scoring the highest on the scholastic aptitude tests. Scabby sits me in the front of the class, telling my mother "he just hasn't been working up to his potential," calling on me all the time like I'm Einstein's little brother. That winter, my father comes to my room, most likely goaded by my mother, and gives me "the talk." It goes something like this: "Uh, Darlin, you may find that once in a while you'll be having a dream and you'll wake up and, um, feel some fluid coming out of your penis. That's called a 'nocturnal emission' and, uh, well, it's not a sin, even though it feels good. So don't worry about it."

My dad has handed down to me the only loophole to pleasure he ever discovered as an Irish Catholic.

It doesn't matter anyway. Despite my suede belt and horseshoe taps, I remain loyal to my grandmother, ignore puberty, deny its urges. I resent my friends as they fall in love, ask girls out, and talk about make-out sessions and the smoothest way to unclasp a bra. When they ignore Scabby's orders and sign up for Mrs. Preble's mixed dance lessons, I am the only one, besides Wendell Joost, whose mother insists on puritanical lessons at Arthur Murray, practicing formal dances with matronly instructors twice my age.

1955: Marin Catholic High School. I switch to desert boots, button-down shirts, ivy-league khakis with a belt in the back. But I'm wary of Elvis' pelvic thrusts. I don't do the be-bop at mixed dances where the girls cover their hickies with makeup and press their lips against their boyfriends' necks. I'm still doing the box step with Wendell and joining the ham radio club. I try out for freshman basketball, but the newly arrived Black kids from Marin City are too good, so I wind up sitting on the bench.

A pretty regular existence, except that I haven't yet held a girl's hand, asked her to the movies, felt her bra strap in a cool back row seat. Through the years I will wonder what my life would have been like if what happened next never occurred. Would I have forgotten my grandmother's warnings about the sins of the flesh and cut loose on the dance floor? Learned to thrust my hips? Would I have been different if circumstance had allowed Desire to call my name and I had felt the intoxicating touch of a girl's lips, the softness of her breasts? Would my fate have changed?

It starts with a cold. Then bright red dots appear on my chest. The next thing I know I'm lying under the bright lights of Marin General Hospital gritting my teeth as they crush my sternum with a needle and suck out the bone marrow to determine what's causing my *idiopathic thrombocytopenic purpura*. My platelet count is 10% of what it should be. My blood isn't coagulating. I feel fine, but they tell me I could get bruised and bleed to death.

I miss two months of school and the cortisone they give me blimps me up like a doughboy. Finally the doctor lets me go back. "No sports of any kind," he says. "Absolutely no fighting and be careful about bumping into things. You could bleed to death." A fat wimp, I waddle back to school and, because there's nothing else to do, I plow into History, Algebra, Latin, English. To my surprise, I enjoy studying. In lieu of a social life, I sign up as the school's sound technician, set up microphones for rallies, run stage lights, play the 45s at school dances. I am a non-combatant on the battlefield of puberty, watching from the sidelines. I'm shocked when, in May, I get elected class president. Vaguely, I wonder if my classmates only voted for me to please the faculty, or worse, because they felt sorry for me.

Father Cornelius Burns takes me under his wing. He is a scholarly young priest whose childhood polio has left him with a limp, causing him to swivel as he carries his huge stack of books under one arm. As my mentor, he teaches me Latin and English, drilling proverbs into my brain. *The weakest ink is stronger than the strongest memory. Repetitio est mater studiorum [Repetition is the mother of studies].* His is a world of immutable essences, absolute truths, apodictic judgments – my grandmother's world.

I spend a lot of time talking to Jesus, asking him why I have this weird blood disease and why I'm so awkward around girls. I'm the only aspiring saint I know and, in the absence of my grandmother, my righteousness is a lonely place. I assume my infirmity is a test to see if I can accept

The Father's will in everything I have no control over – most of my life, it seems.

It's a warm April afternoon during my sophomore year when Father Lacey's voice crackles through the homeroom speakers: "The entrance exam for the seminary will be held this coming Saturday. Anyone interested should sign up in my office in the next two days." I glance around, wondering if anyone in my class will go. Last year Frank Healy did, Bob Murnane the year before that. I saw Frank last month. He said he really liked the seminary's intramural sports program.

That night, I leave my father reading *The Saturday Evening Post* and my mother reading a Flannery O'Connor novel and lie in bed, dozing into a dream. A barely audible but familiar voice draws me out of sleep. *Take the test.* I open my eyes and sit up in bed. Shadows take shape in the dark room. *Jesus.* Jesus wants me to take the test for the seminary. Is this what they mean by a vocation, a calling from God? In the living room, my parents are still reading. They look up, surprised, when I walk in. "I've decided to take the test for the seminary." My mother's eyes search my face. "Well, this is sudden," she says in her schoolteacher's cautioning voice, but I can tell she's pleased. My dad lights up. "By Jove, Darlin', that's wonderful! I think you'll make a damned good priest."

"I might not get accepted, Dad. I'm just going to take the test."

"That's a very sensible approach," my mother says, shooting a glance at my dad who is bubbling with excitement. For years my father has been a member of the Serra Club. Their purpose is to foster priestly vocations. I can tell he's ready to start calling his buddies.

## THE CALL

"They were all good eggs," my father says as we pull into Sacred Heart High School's parking lot that Saturday morning. He is speaking of the others from Marin County who entered the seminary. "It is just that some of them had a vocation," he shrugs and glances sidelong at me, "and some didn't." The San Francisco fog is clearing and in front of us stands the imposing brick building where the exam will be held. I know who my father is referring to, our neighbors Bill Pulskamp and Joey Krause, who dropped out of the seminary after only a couple of years. "Just do your best," he says when I get out of the car. "God will take care of the rest."

Twenty guys are nervously perched on worn desks, talking to one another, or simply looking around, figuring their odds. I search for a common denominator among them, some saintly demeanor perhaps, but they don't look any different from the guys at Marin Catholic, same pimples and peach fuzz. A priest with a pile of booklets comes in and tells us no one is allowed to leave the room except during test section breaks. The longest part will be the Latin. A collective moan rises. The priest laughs.

"Right, that's the toughest, but you have to know your Latin in the seminary."

Three hours later, my face flushed, I walk out to where my dad sits reading the paper in our '53 Chevy. He watches me while he starts the car. "How was it?"

I study the other guys filing out. "Okay I guess. I'm not sure about the Latin."

My dad pulls the car out of the lot. "You remember Father Mariani?" he asks. "His father was an old Italian, sold fertilizer. After Joe entered the seminary, his dad donated a pile of manure to the St. Anslem's festival every year and they'd raffle it off. One of the best fundraisers ever. Seemed everybody in Marin wanted manure."

My dad pushes in the lighter and re-lights his cigar. With a shot of panic I realize he's assuming I will pass with great scores, go to the seminary and become a priest. He is counting on it, as one counts on outliving his parents, on summer fog in San Francisco; he's counting on his only son making him proud, never making a wrong or foolish turn. I close my eyes. Unbidden, all those Latin words come swimming into my mind.

"You heard from the seminary yet?" Gerry O'Donnell, my cynical, snobbish English teacher, who up until now has never paid much attention to me, has beckoned me up after class. "Not yet," I tell him. He looks at me up and down as though I'm wearing a particularly classy suit. "Well, let me know," he says. He pushes his hand out to me to shake it. In the lunch line Mike Gallagher, one of the wildest, most popular, guys in our class, slaps me on the back and says, "I just want you to know, I think you'll make a great priest. We really need good priests. I could never do it myself, so good luck." Francine Rogers, a cheerleader I was sure didn't know I existed, bounces up to me in the hall and says, "Hey Greg, I hear you're going to the seminary. That's great." I've become some kind of hero, riding off into a seminary sunset. It feels good, this respect, this sudden intimacy.

I stand in the kitchen one Friday afternoon in June with the seminary letter in my hand. No one else is around. My heart is beating fast. The letter says I passed the test, they have already informed my pastor. I will receive more information soon. I look out into the backyard where my grandfather's Eden blooms. I think about my grandmother in her rocker, her arthritic hands running through the rosary, condemning Liz Peck for whistling, then suddenly dying, without saying goodbye.

On our Saturday shopping trip, my father tells all the checkers at Guasco's market, the lady at the dry cleaners, and Harry Mueller at the hardware. I stare at my shoes on the linoleum floor, feel the hot flush on my cheeks and wish my father would quit saying my name. On the way home, I watch the oak trees blurring past. "Lots of guys get in," I say into the Chevy's stale air. "That doesn't mean they make it through all twelve years." My father leans over and pats my knee. "Don't worry about a thing, Darlin'. You're going to do just fine."

The next week another letter arrives. You have been officially accepted into St. Joseph's, the words read. There's a pamphlet enclosed called <u>The Little City of God</u> by Father Lyman A. Fenn. "*St Joseph's College is the little 'City of God,' complete in itself, standing isolated against the 'City of the World,' having within its limits and independent of 'that other city,' all the means and possibilities to equip young citizens for their future warfare against the 'City of Confusion.'*" I like this. It conjures up my grandmother's worldview, that clear and righteous warrior perspective. "*Constant self-surrender which leads to abiding self-control, is the keynote of his character building; not the modern self-improvement or progress.*" Spiritual bootcamp, I think. Just what I need. I've been worried lately that if I don't get more focused on my spiritual life I might end up in Hell.

That summer, I shed my wimp status and work at the high school for a dollar an hour, watering plants, re-coding locker combinations, varnishing desks. There's a crew of us. I'm cleaning lockers with Mike Anderson and he's telling me he wants to buy an old chevy, fix it up. A minute later he's confiding in me he might go into the seminary after high school. Jack McGuinness, our 23 year-old crew leader, is driving me out to water the baseball field. Out of the blue he says, "Y'know? I really wish I could live a better life." As if I'm his father or something. I walk home that afternoon along the dusty path next to Egger's nursery. What if I don't stay in the seminary? What if God really isn't calling me to the priesthood? What will my dad think then? I stare at the shrubs lined up inside the fence, imagining my grandmother peering down from her Heavenly rocking chair, watching me like a hawk, making sure I don't fall prey to the sin of pride.

When I get home a packet from the seminary is lying on the table. Inside are sew-on laundry numbers, #174. All my clothing has to have 174 on it. Except my socks, which will be washed in a nylon mesh bag woven shut with a diaper pin stamped 174. I read down the list of required items: shoe shine kit, dust mop, broom, waste basket, drinking glass, spoon, rug, chest of drawers. In the afternoons, Mrs. Pulskamp comes over and sits in my grandmother's old rocker. She and my mother sew 174s on all my things. "Bill went in too early," she tells my mother, "right out of the eighth grade. He only lasted a year. I told Jim he's going to have to wait until after high school." She rips thread with her teeth. I've never heard Jim say anything about wanting to enter the seminary.

After a couple of weeks, I begin to identify with 174. It's a tall, thin number, more angular than round, long limbed. I begin collecting the items on the list as if they were hallowed ceremonial objects. A footnote says nothing can be hung on the walls, the chest can't exceed four drawers, all our clothes must be *conservative in color* and design. My father and his Serra Club friends give me their drabbest coats, jackets and ties, and I assume this is part of becoming a man of the cloth.

Late in the summer Bob Murnane and I speed around the hills of Marin in the little Hillman his father has lent him for the summer. I ask anxious seminary questions between screeching turns and Bob assures me that I'll like it there. "The classes are tough and the rules are strict, but we still have a lot of fun." Judging by his driving, the seminary has unleashed something wild in Bob and I wonder about that. We're roaring down Wolfe Grade now. "You'll get drafted on one of four teams and play baseball, soccer, basketball, track and swimming. Everybody's on a team and everyone has to play." My heart starts pounding with excitement as I think about playing sports again. My folks are still worried about me bleeding to death, but I've decided if God's calling me to the seminary He must also be calling me back to sports as well. What my folks don't know won't hurt them.

## ANSWERING THE CALL

September arrives and the San Francisco Seals finally win the Pacific Coast League pennant, only to be exiled to Phoenix to make room for a major league team in San Francisco. I'm hoping for the Dodgers, but it turns out to be the Giants instead. My dad tells me that Senator Joe McCarthy, "a good Catholic boy," has been killed by the Commies, driven to a heart attack by their smear tactics. Times are bad. I'm glad I'm going into the seminary.

Our green '53 Chevy is in the driveway, stuffed with my dresser, mop, rug, drab clothes, drinking glass, spoon, shoeshine kit – everything dutifully checked off the list we received at the beginning of the summer. I squeeze into the front between my mom and dad and my grandfather wedges himself between the mop and the chest of drawers in the back. It's hot in Marin, but we run into a chilly fog on the Golden Gate Bridge and it lasts until we get to El Camino Real south of the city. The air warms up along the peninsula and gets uncomfortably hot and dusty by the time we reach the Grant Road turnoff in Mountain View. We meander through acres and acres of fruit trees and finally turn down a little road marked St. Joseph's Avenue that winds through a stand of eucalyptus before narrowing into a hedge-bordered lane. At the end of the lane a brick building looms, fronted by a large grassy circle with palm trees. We follow the arrow along the right side of the circle until we reach the front of the building, four stories high with an elegant bell tower extending another two stories. I remember Father Fenn's description in <u>The Little City of God</u>: *The building has a certain severity of outline, unavoidable in an architecture designedly stout.* This is no frat house.

As we pull up in front of the stairs, an older student in a black suit approaches us with a clipboard. He finds my name on the list and reads off a room number, pointing up to the third floor. "You're allowed to use the elevator in the front hall, but only for your dresser. Usually it's off limits. And you can't bring the dresser up the front stairs here. You have to drive around to the side. Everything else you'll have to carry up the side stairs."

We can handle stairs. My dad's a young 71 and my grandfather's definitely spry for 87. We have stairs at home. We drive around the building and wrestle the dresser up a short flight of stairs then down a long corridor to the elevator. We ride up to the third floor, then carry it down another long corridor around the corner to number 34. The door is open, revealing a compact 7' x 10' room with twin bed, hinged shoe-shine box, chair, wash basin and built-in medicine chest. The small closet is empty. Out the high window I can see our guide giving directions to another family. Luckily the staircase is closer to my room than the elevator was.

After about three trips my grandfather is huffing and puffing. "Dad, sit down on the bed and rest," my mother tells him, and he does.

Other guys are moving in too. I watch as my dad hefts a suitcase up the stairs, my mother carries the broom, mop and crocheted rug, her permed curls beginning to droop with sweat, and suddenly I feel vulnerable, protective of my little band of elders.

My mother makes my bed, hangs my clothes in the closet, fills the medicine chest. I'm starting to wish they'd leave, but I also don't want them to. My mom straightens the bedspread one more time, then brushes her hands together. "I think it's time for us to go so you can settle in." She gives me a brusque hug. "I love you dear." My dad gives me a wet kiss holding fast to my shoulders. When he stands back to look at me I see his pale blue eyes blinking back tears. "If you need anything, Darlin', just let us know." Grandad hangs back as usual, then grabs my hand as they're walking out the door. His chiseled features are taut, as when Mayme died. "Do good, Greggie," he tells me. I open the door and we head down the hall. At the car my mom grabs me one more time and hugs me so tightly I can't move. My grandad wipes his glasses and looks away. "It's only three weeks 'til visiting Sunday," my dad says, forcing a smile. "We'll see you then."

The Chevy moves away and I think about my mom getting up the next morning, passing my empty room, missing me at the breakfast table. This Saturday, Dad will run the errands by himself and Grandad will smoke alone in the basement gazing up at my jerry-rigged ham radio lines. The tail lights are almost out of sight when I turn around and head back toward the brick building to my new world. While I'm climbing up to my room, I realize that three flights is a lot of stairs.

## FIRST IMPRESSIONS

As I pass the room next to mine, I see a guy with sandy hair and glasses hanging a suit in his closet. "Hi," I say. "My name's Greg. I live next door." He turns around smiling and walks over to me, hand extended. "Hey, nice to meetcha. I'm Dick Ormsby." His voice is resonant, reassuring. "You must be a *non-orig.*"

His handshake is soft but sure. "What's a *non-orig?*" I ask.

"It means you must have transferred in from outside. I'm what's called an orig, an original, because I entered right out of eighth grade. All it means is you probably had more fun. Let me get this stuff put away and I'll show you around."

There's more activity in the halls now, latecomers arriving, greeting each other. Then a rich tenor voice, floating above all the others, is singing in a cockney accent. "*All I want is a room somewhere, far away from the cold night air.*" Dick laughs. "That's Bob Carroll. He's a theater buff, probably seen every play and movie ever made. Sounds as though he liked *My Fair Lady.*" I look out in the corridor and see a light complexioned redhead with a sharp nose and dancing blue eyes. Dick introduces us. Bob reminds me of a bird, timid but also aggressive.

Dick takes me downstairs, showing me the classrooms and the huge study hall that we share with the class ahead of us. "We don't call them *seniors* like you do outside. It's *first high* through *fourth high*. Then, once you're in college, you're *Poets* and *Rhets*. Another name for *first high* guys is *sixth Latiners*, because they have six years of Latin ahead of them." A bulletin board outside the study hall displays the daily schedule and the dining room seating assignments. I'm glad to see Dick and I are at the same table.

Everyone is starting to gather in the central courtyard, anticipating the dinner bell. We walk through the crowd, Dick introducing me to his friends. Some seem excited to be back, others are grumbling about summer ending too fast. My brain is spinning wildly, trying to reconcile this wild array of characters with my former stereotype of seminarians. By now there are about 300 guys in the courtyard and the noise is getting intense. "Hey, Mannion, who's going to win this year?"

"Not the Trojans."

"The Ramblers!"

Dick steers us in and out of groups, favoring, I notice, the quieter, more serious guys rather than the loud jock types. We meet Conrad Gruber and Al Larkin, Steve Matosich and Pete Martinez, Ed Gaffney and Gerry Winkenbach, all of them very friendly and welcoming. Then we run into a guy, ambling along like a mob boss, decked out in white bucks and a sports jacket, surrounded by a bunch of rawboned jock types. Dick doesn't seem as sure of himself now. "Uh, Greg, this is Mike McLaughlin, another classmate of ours." McLaughlin gives me a half-hearted handshake, looking over my shoulder, playing the crowd. Out of the corner of his mouth, he mumbles, "What parish ya from?"

"St. Sebastian's. In Kentfield."

"Marin, eh? I used to play ball with a guy from Marin." He mentions a name, still looking over my shoulder.

"I've heard of him," I say, "but I never really met him."

He and his sidekicks are already moving on. "Nice to meetcha, Mike," I call after him. Nothing.

"He's the assistant captain of the Trojans," Dick says. "He's a jock."

"Not very friendly," I say.

"Not in a group, but he's okay by himself." Dick doesn't sound very convinced.

At exactly 5:57 the Angelus bell sounds and the courtyard cacophony goes silent. I look around and see a few seminarians with their eyes closed moving their lips in silent prayer. Others are glancing around, shooting furtive smiles at friends. The bell tolls on, then everyone walks rapidly, silently, toward the dining room, which Dick told me is called the refectory.

I follow Dick into a large room with high ceilings, beige walls and dark paneling. Long tables are covered with shiny clear plastic over white cotton tablecloths. Dick gestures me to a chair across from him and we stand in silence with the others. Off to one side is a raised platform where the members of the faculty stand like deities on Mt. Olympus. When everyone is in place, Fr. Campbell, the rector, says something in Latin and the entire community barks something back in a single voice. I wonder what they're saying and again experience old fears about my inadequacies in Latin.

The prayer finished, everyone sits down, still in silence, and an older student climbs stairs to a pulpit set high at one end of the refectory. Very methodically he opens the Bible and begins reading from the New Testament, pronouncing each word distinctly and carefully. This seems like serious business. He's certainly not sacrificing enunciation for expression. The reading ends in the same pained precision it started, and, after a moment of silence, the rector says *"Tu autem, Domine, miserere nobis."*

*"Deo Gratias!"* the assembly yells and everyone starts talking at once. There are nine guys sitting at our table. "I'm Rich Mangini," says the neatly dressed, well-combed guy at the head of the table. "Your tablehead. You can call me Mange." He picks up his fork and points it at Dick. "Dick's my right-hand man, his job is to cut the meat into nine perfectly" – he raises his eyebrows at Dick as though already scolding him – "equal pieces and pass them down. What's your name?" pointing the fork at me.

"Greg."

"Well, Greg, you're my *left-hand man*. You have to cut the mystery. That's dessert. We usually don't know what it is, so we call it *mystery*. You," he points to the guy next to me and then to the one across from him, "you are the butter cutters; your job is to draw a nine-part grid on the butter. Which we call *grease*." He points further down the line and I wonder how long this lesson will last, when we'll get to eat. "You're the milk pourers," Mange says to the next set of diners. "You can get more milk by holding up the pitcher for one of the waiters. You should try to get seconds on everything, but you always have a better chance with milk or potatoes than with meat or mystery. You guys at the bottom of the table," he calls. "You're the pilers. Your job is to scrape all the leftovers into that bottom pan, pile up all the dirty dishes, and then sort the dirty silverware in the other pan." Mange sits back, sets his fork on his plate. "We all started as pilers," he says, "so I don't want to hear any complaining."

When it's time for dessert, I slice through a gooey chocolate cake-like affair knowing one slip of the knife will set the whole table howling, though it will be the left-hand piler who really suffers, since he'll get stuck with the last, presumably smallest, piece of this strange concoction.

"If any of you start screwing around," Mange tells us as he watches me cut, "or if you challenge my authority, all I have to do is stand up, and the Prefect of Discipline will be down here just like that."

Ormsby turns to the butter cutter on his right, laughing. "Remember when Tobin stood up on Maloney last year?" The butter cutter nods. "Yeah. Poor Phil."

The bell rings at the end of the meal and everyone goes silent again. The reader climbs back up to the pulpit and reads a passage from <u>The Imitation of Christ</u> by Thomas a'Kempis. Father Campbell follows it with another prayer in Latin. "*Amen*" the student body calls in unison, and we all rise and head for the door. People seem to be shaking hands as they go out. When we get to the door, Dick reaches over, dips his right hand into a holy water font and extends it to me. I touch his moist fingers with the tips of my own and make the sign of the cross as the others are doing. "This used to be the chapel before they built the new wing two years ago," Dick says. "That's why the fonts are still here."

Outside in the cool September air we join Conrad Gruber and Al Larkin and walk down the service road past the swimming pool toward the old barn that houses the indoor basketball courts. On the way we pass other groups of walkers, some of whom trade barbs with each other like rival armies. "Different teams," Dick explains. He and Conrad and Al talk about the faculty, the courses and other classmates, but not much about sports.

After half an hour we return to the chapel for the rosary, then walk in silence to the study hall where Father Campbell sits, pink and globular, on a raised dais, holding a copy of *The Seminary Rule*. He looks down at us through his round, wire-rimmed glasses. "This," he says, "is your path to holiness. *The Rule* spells out God's will for you every moment of the day." I begin to feel more comfortable. This is one challenge I can meet. I don't know if I can make it as a scholar or an athlete, but I can definitely follow rules.

At 5:50 the next morning I'm ripped from sleep by the blaring electric bell Father Campbell has dubbed *vox dei,* the voice of God. Moments later someone bangs on my door yelling something in Latin. When I open it, he's already down the hall, banging on other doors, repeating the same Latin phrase. I pull on my pants and t-shirt and hurry down to the bathroom. Silent classmates stumble in and out of the stalls like zombies. I'm still fumbling with my tie as I run down the stairs into the cold darkness of the courtyard. The cavernous chapel echoes with muffled sounds of kneelers being lifted, students squeezing into pews. McLaughlin kneels next to me, his butt resting on the pew.

At communion time, we all stand and the kid on the aisle raises the kneeler with his foot so we can file out of the pew. As we're coming back, someone in the row ahead kicks our kneeler and it whacks Mike Hearney right on the shins. Everyone starts giggling.

The grand silence ends at breakfast with an explosion of voices. Mange is the only guy at our table whose hair is perfectly combed, tie flawless. He waves his knife like a baton. "Today is Thursday, our weekly holiday, so we don't have any classes. You new guys are supposed to go down to the campus and play softball. That way the scouts can look you over and decide whether they want to pick you. We're all on a team. I'm a Rambler." He gestures at Dick. "He's an Indian. Everyone has to play." Mange stabs his fork into the scrambled eggs. "And you can't hold out."

"What do you mean *hold out*?" I say.

He looks at me, chewing his eggs carefully. "A couple of years ago two new guys pretended they didn't know how to play softball. They kept dropping flies and throwing like girls, so nobody thought they were any good. Turns out the Trojan captain put them up to it because he was from their parish in Oakland and knew how good they were. He was able to wait until the third or fourth round to pick them. That's why the Trojans ended up with all the best athletes in that class. They cheated."

As he talks, my heart starts beating faster. Am I ready to play sports? These guys are out for blood and I've been on the bench for two years. With a blood disease.

## THE RULE

Classes start the next day. Father Olivier's black hair is parted perfectly, his cassock is spotless "*Quo usque tandem abutere, Catilina, patientia nostra,*" he intones and panic grips me, but luckily, he calls on Tom Sheehan. "Show us how it's done." Tom skates smoothly through the next few lines of Cicero's convoluted Latin. What am I doing in this class? Why didn't they put me in the "B" group where I belong? Jack Olivier extends a finely manicured hand toward Al Potter. "Alex, continue please." Potter crashes through the next passage, furiously thumbing through his dictionary as he goes. These guys are amazing, extracting meaning from what to me is still just a series of words. I'm okay at translating individual phrases and recognizing verb forms. But actually making sense of whole sentences and paragraphs? No way.

"Mr. McAllister. How do they do it at Marin Catholic?" I want to say, "Not very well," but I'm so terrified I just stare at the sentence in front of me. Finally I begin translating, a word at a time.

"I don't think Cicero would put it quite that way." The rest of the class laughs, relieved. I'm going to pose no threat to them.

English class next with Father Taylor. He hobbles in with a cane, eases himself gingerly into his chair, and glances at us as though he resents our presence. Pursing his lips, he speaks and then snorts, kick-starting his nose every few words. "All right, okay (snort). You will write several essays in this class (snort) and they will be thoroughly critiqued (snort)." He swivels his chair, grabs a piece of chalk, and writes on the blackboard: *A nickname is a sign of affection.* "This is your first (snort) assignment. Three hundred words please (snort), double spaced."

Nicknames are common in the seminary, especially for the faculty, and nicknames aren't always a sign of affection. His is *Larry*, but the guys who don't like him call him *The Gimp*. Everyone calls Father Campbell *Beansy* behind his back. I wonder if Larry has given us this assignment to learn our secrets.

In Greek class, Father Perkowski comes in looking like a deer in the headlights. He's young and freshly minted from a seminary back East. He leads us in sing-song recitations of noun and verb forms, keeping the beat with a thumbs-up fist. *"Ho potamos, tou potamou!"* He's probably our easiest teacher. He's also my confessor and I think of him as guileless and saintly, like me.

Father Conner teaches us speech. We call him Doc because that's what he calls everyone else. "Put it in the bone, Doc," he says over and over. The "bone" is the sphenoid cavity, Doc's favorite part of the body. "The sphenoid is where you get the volume and pitch you'll need to read in the refectory," Doc tells us.

We have four study hall periods a day. "Evening study periods should be devoted to Latin and English classes," Beansy tells us. "In the other study periods, you should prepare for the classes that immediately follow." McLaughlin sits next to me in study hall and I watch him furtively reading numbers from last year's Trojan record book when he should be studying. He's in the B group, so I assume his classes aren't as hard as mine. Every Wednesday night in the weeks to come, McLaughlin will ask me if he can borrow a stamp for a letter home. "I'll pay you back," he says. But he never does.

After dinner Beansy drones away from the elevated platform. Sitting at my desk, I wonder why they call this *spiritual* reading? All he's doing is reading *The Rule* of the seminary at us. He's short and round with a resemblance to the Campbell soup kid. As I listen to him spouting rules in his high-pitched voice, I picture Tubby Moffitt's clubhouse in the Little Lulu comic books. "No girls allowed" is scribbled on the side.

*"Rings and similar ornamentation, as well as faddish haircuts, are forbidden."* Beansy runs his pudgy fingers through his few strands of unkempt hair. *"Card playing, gambling, hazing, and football are forbidden."* Football? What's wrong with football? *"Students are forbidden to have radios. All letters must be placed in the mail box unsealed. Incoming mail will be inspected by the Reverend Superior before delivery."* I imagine Beansy at his desk, buried under a huge pile of letters from mothers. I need to remind my folks to be careful what

they write.

It's nine-thirty at night and the lights-out bell has just rung. I kneel next to my bed and pray one more time before going to sleep. We've prayed at least thirty times already today, and that's not even counting Mass, meditation, spiritual reading and the rosary. Those were all formal prayers, most of them in Latin. Now I'm just talking to Jesus, going over the day. I feel calm and peaceful, just he and I alone in the dark.

My door flies open with a bang and my head jerks up. My insides go cold. Father Canfield is standing in my threshold, silhouetted against the corridor lights. "What are you doing, son?"

"Uh, saying my night prayers, Father."

"It's lights-out, son. You should be in bed."

The door closes. Soft padded footsteps recede down the hall. I've heard stories of Cat Canfield, how he prowls the corridors at night looking for students breaking *The Rule*. Thank goodness I wasn't reading under the covers with a flashlight, or dangling a transistor radio antenna out my window, or, Jeez, standing there naked. I slip into bed, shaking. Jesus tells me he's sorry for getting me in trouble, says we'll talk tomorrow.

Next morning at breakfast I tell Mange and Dick about Cat's visit. "Yeah," Dick says, "you never know when he's going to turn up. Even if you have your door locked, he can get his key in, turn it, and whip it open all in one motion."

"And you never want to leave anything incriminating in

your room," Mange says. "Last year Cat found a paperback novel hung on a hanger under some guy's suit pants. Two hours later he got a bus ticket home."

"For reading a book?"

Mange shrugs. "It wasn't approved."

I nod. The truth is, I want my superiors to be strong, I want them to be wise. I have the idea that the more elderly they are, the more they know and the more respect they deserve. I've noticed the same classmates who flout *The Rule* also ridicule the faculty and I find this somehow upsetting. Did they never have elderly people living in their household? Coming out of the refectory after breakfast, I hear McLaughlin and Cunningham making fun of the old priest they call *The Floater* who inches his walker along the cloister, grey bearded, his wispy long hair disheveled, his eyes deep in sunken sockets. He stops and sits down on his walker seat, staring off like an Old Testament prophet. Surely some wisdom resides behind that weathered visage, I think. I try to catch his eye when we walk past, but he doesn't respond.

Until one morning, a few days later, I'm lagging behind the rest, late for class and hoping to God my Latin's done right, and he beckons me with a long crooked finger. I look around to see, is he talking to me?

I walk up to him. "Hi, Father," I say.

He beckons me closer.

I lean down, see the dried soup and bread crumbs in his beard and put my ear near his cracked lips, hoping to catch his fragile revelation. The lips move and a guttural sound emerges, borne on the foulest breath: "Aaargh."

I stagger back some. "What did you say, Father?" His grey rheumy eyes regard me with a fierce look.

"Aaargh," he says again.

I stand there for a minute, waiting for Jesus to enlighten me, to decipher the aaargh into something sacred and meaningful. Finally, not knowing what else to do, I raise my hand in short farewell and jog back toward class.

Royal B. Webster, *The Floater*, remains a mystery.

## TEMPTATIONS

The annual four-day retreat starts a week later. "This is our time to re-commit ourselves to our vocations." Father Ring is the spit-polished retreat-master. "Remember, you are preparing to become *Other Christs*. You must die to your selves daily by obedient submission to your superiors." He paces back and forth across the marble sanctuary, his shiny black shoes echoing dramatically in the high-ceilinged chapel, his black hair glistening in the shaft of morning sun filtering through stained glass windows. "A superior may err in commanding, but you will never err in obeying."

Each day he hammers out a different theme, moving us toward his theatrical finale. On the last day, he stands in the middle of the sanctuary in silence, head bowed. Slowly he looks up at us. "Whenever you are tempted, men — and tempted you shall be — consider the consequences. Eternal Hellfire, licking mercilessly at your raw, scorched, never-decomposing flesh. Unbearable agony, Gentlemen, unquenchable thirst. And for what? For one illicit pleasure, one prideful act, one momentary slip, you must endure the excruciating pain of Hellfire for eternity."

Not a sound in the chapel.

"Eternity, Gentlemen, is a long time. Imagine if Mount Everest, the largest mountain in the world were made of solid steel. Once a year a tiny hummingbird flies by and, ever so lightly, brushes this mountain of steel with her wing." His voice goes deeper, his eyes burn, and a spiked finger drives each word into our pliant brains. Shouting now: "Gentleman, the length of time it would take that hummingbird to wear away Mount Everest... that is only the BEGINNING of eternity!"

Absolute silence. No one moves. The retreat master bows his head, makes the sign of the cross, and walks toward the foot of the altar. Four hundred of us are riveted to our pews by images of flames and angry Gods, steel mountains and scorched hummingbirds. No rules will be broken that day.

That night Beansy reminds us that tomorrow is visiting Sunday. "You are allowed to entertain your guests on the lawn or along the service road, but don't bring them inside." I try to imagine Beansy as a young seminarian on visiting Sundays. Were his parents also rotund, Campbell soup people?

After lunch the next day, we emerge like celebrities through the seminary's big front doors. I scan the crowd gathered outside. Picnic tables dot the lawn, cars line the roads. Younger siblings run to hug their black-clad brothers. Parents tentatively approach sons no longer exclusively theirs. I catch sight of my mom and dad standing off to one side, gently out of place in this noisy group. I hurry toward them.

"Hi Mom." She hugs me and the scent of her familiar perfume brings me warm relief. She continues to hold me tightly and kisses my forehead quickly, then leans back so she can look me up and down, her blue eyes moist, her fingers gripping my upper arms. She looks flower fresh, delicate in her stylish pillbox hat. "I think you've grown some," she says spinning me around to show my father. He's standing there grinning, his Stetson perched rakishly on his head. Highlighted against a sea of pulsing young families, he stands as a jaunty symbol of a more seasoned generation. I feel the odd vertigo that comes from merging two very different worlds. My dad steps forward. "We sure are proud of you, Darlin'." He hugs me, plants a wet kiss on my lips. The vague scent of his cigar warms my heart and I close my eyes and feel everything else melt away: the seminary rules, the classes I'm working so hard in, the endless prayers, McLaughlin and his stamps, the cold morning bell, and all those nights that are absent of my parents, knowing they are sitting in the living room, reading and watching television while I drift off to sleep. "You're sure missed around the old homestead," he says, tousling my hair. His pale blue eyes crinkle into another smile and his left eyebrow goes up. "Especially by that little dog of yours."

"I'll bet you're hungry," my mother says. "Grandad's over there guarding the food." She points toward the lawn and we move that way. I see my grandfather sitting in a patio chair, white shirt rolled to the elbows, brown fedora shading his shiny cheekbones, suit jacket folded across his lap. We eat fried chicken, Mrs. Pulskamp's homemade pumpkin pie. I tell them everything about the seminary, point out friends and classmates. Paul Feyen walks by with his family. "Hey Greg," he says, I'd like you to meet my folks and my sisters, Ann and Jean." I shake their hands and introduce him to my folks. While they talk, I glance back at Ann. She meets my gaze with intelligent, laughing eyes. I feel a little flutter and turn away.

At 4:15 the bell rings. "Well, I guess that's your call," my mother says with just a hint of irritation. She stands and picks up her napkin that has fallen to the ground. My dad and grandfather both get up too, as though obeying some old religious prompt from childhood. I look over at the table and see the scattered remains of chicken and pie. Three hours ago the table was full, brimming with anticipated delights. We were too. My dad sets his soggy cigar next to the plate of chicken bones and wraps his hands around mine. "Nice to see you, Darlin'." He kisses me with moist lips. Behind him my mother watches us. She dabs her eyes with her napkin. "Don't forget to write," my dad tells me. "We'll see you next month." My grandfather is standing back, turning his straw hat with rough fingers. "Goodbye, Grandad," I say walking toward him. He shakes my hand, then gives me a tentative hug. "Good boy," he says. My mother hugs me too tightly, then lets go and shoos me toward the other black-clad figures who are heading toward the building, turning, waving back. I walk resolutely toward the door and only turn at the last minute. The three of them stand in a line, my dad's arm around my mother's shoulder. My grandfather still holds his hat in one hand, the faint breeze blowing his few grey hairs straight up. They all wave one last time.

I re-enter the building visualizing the three of them packing up the picnic table and driving off, missing me. Putting on cassocks and surplices we are, all of us, subdued. No one says much. We head to the chapel for Compline. The cantor's voice shatters the silence: *Fratres, sobrii estote et vigilate.* We attempt to wrench our spirits back from the distractions of food and family. *Brothers, be sober and watchful,* sings the cantor, *for thy enemy the devil, like a raging lion, goeth about seeking whom he may devour.* Have I been tempted that afternoon? Has my encounter with the world weakened my spiritual resolve? What about Paul's cute sister? I glance at McLaughlin next to me and see him examining his nails behind his hymnal. He doesn't seem to worry about temptation as much as my grandmother and I.

"Hey McAllister!" Jack O'Shea catches up to me as I'm coming out of chapel. "You want to go on a walk next Thursday?" "Sure," I tell him, honored to be included. "Great." He waves a hand and heads off. "I gotta get 15 guys signed up in order to go off campus." I stand there looking at him. Well, at least I was one of the fifteen he asked.

Thursday afternoon we meet outside Cat Canfield's office. Fourteen guys in their flashiest, just barely conservative, clothes, their hair combed back, line up single file outside Cat's door. "Do I line up too?" I whisper to Dick.

"Is Cat holding smokes for you?" he asks.

Canfield opens his door. Guys go in one by one and emerge with packs of cigarettes, pipes and cigars that have been in storage since the beginning of the year. They affix them as accessories, wrapping them in the sleeves of T-shirts, dangling them unlit between their teeth, tucking them over an ear. James Dean as seminarian. "Last year, in second high," Dick tells me, "we weren't allowed to smoke on walks." This year we're a pluming locomotive. Nervous Mountain View housewives peer through Venetian blinds to watch this curious gaggle of Marlboro men chugging through their neighborhood.

Loyola Corners is a small shopping center with a drug store, café, and other small businesses. *The Rule* forbids us from eating in restaurants, buying magazines, and listening to rock music. I go over to the drug store and buy some toothpaste. Walking back, I try to ignore John Cunningham and the others sitting around a table in the café, eating hamburgers and reading Time Magazine, *Blue Suede Shoes* blaring from the jukebox. I know if you're going to commit yourself to God, you should go all the way, not cut corners like that, and *The Rule* says we're supposed to practice fraternal correction and report our classmates to our confessor if we see them doing something immoral. But breaking the rule isn't exactly immoral. It's just … lax. My confessor, Father Perkowsky, wouldn't know what to do about it anyway, it would just make him more nervous. Face flushed, I hurry on, suppressing the holier-than-thou judgments that would isolate me from my peers, wishing things were different, that I could be more cool.

## SPORTS

The locker room already smells like old socks even though it's the first week of the year. I stand at my locker trying not to show my skinny white legs as I pull on my sweats. "*BOs*," Dick told me last night, "we don't call them sweats." I watch McLaughlin next to me as he pulls a red baseball shirt over his muscled chest and laces up his mean-looking spikes. He adjusts a red baseball hat on his carefully combed hair, checks his reflection in a small mirror hanging inside his locker, then saunters out, spikes echoing on the tile floor. I grab my lumpy old baseball mitt and follow him. The field is down on the other side of the creek, an old meadow that's been broken into three baseball diamonds. The morning fog still glistens on the grass as the team captains huddle with their scouts to one side, watching us. McLaughlin is whispering something into Jersey Joe Harrington's ear. I stand with the other new guys, kneading my glove nervously, trying to push images of parents and doctors out of my mind. When I hear my name called, I run out to join the others on team B. Later I walk up to the plate, plant my feet, swing the bat a few times looking for the old rhythm. I watch a couple of pitches then swing at one coming in high and outside. The bat connects sending the ball into shallow right field. I scramble toward first, unfamiliar muscles waking up, laughing in my legs. I cross the bag, relieved. No collisions, no plasma explosions so far. A big kid with acne comes up next, hits a long ball over the left fielder's head. I round the bases and score. Winded, I stand behind the backstop with my hands on my knees, catching my breath. McLaughlin sidles up to me. Moving in close, he checks his clipboard and talks out of the side of his mouth like we're planning a drug deal.

"Ever play any ball at Marin Catholic?"

"No," I say. "I got a blood disease my Freshman year and couldn't play sports."

He lifts an eyebrow, looks at me over his glasses.

" A disease?"

He makes a mark on his clipboard and walks away. Three days later there's a mob around the bulletin board where they've posted the draft results. I worm my way in and scan the names. I'm not listed in the Trojan column – no surprise after McLaughlin's scouting report – nor under Bears or Ramblers. I'm an Indian, last year's worst team. "Anybody know who was first pick?" a kid asks.

"Conneely," a chorus of voices replies. He's the sixth-latiner who's been charging the senior stairs every day, trying to fight his way to the top while we're waiting for mail-call after lunch. A scrappy little guy, he comes back day after day even though he's gotten several *jake shampoos*. Yesterday I watched him in the locker room, kicking and yelling while the bigger guys stuck his head in the toilet and flushed it. He came out red-faced but still laughing, calling them chickenshits.

After supper Pat Browne gives me a little jerk of his head. "Let's take a walk." He jams his hands in the pockets of his windbreaker as he leads me away from the crowd. A tall good-looking kid, Pat usually hangs around with the jocks, acting cool. Why's he taking a walk with me?

Once we're out of earshot of the others, he flashes a smile. "You got picked on the Indians. It's a good team." He walks slowly, talking in short, clipped sentences. "We've got a shot at it this year. If Conneely doesn't get his ass thrown out, we'll win the peanut division. MacNamara's the best basketball player in our class, except maybe for Brady. So we'll do okay in basketball. Baseball we're strong. I pitch and Potter catches. You might play first base. Soccer's our weakest sport. Healy's our only really good player. We need a goalie, so that might be your job."

"How do you play soccer? I've never even heard of it."

"I really don't like it that much. The faculty makes us play it because that's what they played over in France. Basically, you run around and kick each other."

Pat keeps talking and I start to get a *déjà vu* of times spent with my Grandmother, when she used to catalog the neighbors for me, telling me who was going to Heaven and who was doomed to Hell. Except Pat phrases things differently. "Mac's a good ball player," "Leary's an asshole," "Sullivan's pretty funny," "Johnson doesn't know his ass from his elbow." I'm glad we're on the same team.

Softball season starts and lots of guys show up in their old CYO baseball shirts and spikes. I imagine them being coached on well-manicured San Francisco playgrounds while I was dodging gopher holes on neighborhood sandlots, and I start to worry that I won't be able to compete. But then the game starts and half the guys turn out to be terrible athletes. They're only playing because *The Rule* demands it.

Softball season is only a month, then the weather turns colder and it's time for soccer. "I'm going to start you as goalie," says John Van Hagen, consulting his rain-soaked clipboard. "All you have to do is stop the ball from going between the posts."

Yeah, sure, easy for him to say. Last week Frank Healy gave me the lowdown. "Soccer's where everyone works out their aggressions on each other. It used to be football, but too many guys broke their collarbones so they outlawed it." After watching McLaughlin lace up his battle-scarred football cleats and slide cardboard shin guards behind his knee socks, all I can imagine is getting kicked and bleeding to death right there in the goal box. The field is muddy for our first game and the early morning air frigid. My hands are stiff and I'm worried that the ball will bounce right off them. There's no such thing as an offside rule in seminary soccer, so the other team is always swarming around me waiting for the ball to arrive. My only protection is my fullbacks, Pat Browne and Al Potter, and after a few plays I realize why Pat doesn't like soccer; he doesn't like contact. He just runs toward the kicker, then ducks away at the last minute and yells, "Get 'im Potts!" Al is more gutsy, he actually charges the kicker, but half the time he misses the ball completely, leaving me at the mercy of McLaughlin and his waffle-iron boots. I don't do well the first few games, but gradually I get the hang of it and after a few good saves my teammates nickname me *Spider*, which I take as a sign of affection.

After Christmas, soccer gives way to basketball. An old barn has been converted into two narrow courts. I can see my breath as I warm up for the first game against Denny O'Brien and the Ramblers. Mike MacNamara's our star player, so I just rebound and pass him the ball. Bob Carroll and Poopsy Perry are no help under the basket, though Bob cracks a lot of funny jokes. The courts are filthy. The dust is so bad I end up with a nose full of muddy snot by the end of the first quarter. The Ramblers start double-teaming MacNamara, so I have to shoot once in a while. I'm a lousy shot. Our other squad is better balanced. Both Browne and Potter are good shooters. The problem is they both love to shoot, so they always end up fighting with each other over the ball. Other teams come to their games just to watch them cuss at each other.

Even though regular football is outlawed, we're allowed to play a non-blocking form of it called *"Chuckball."* A few of us play it for fun between regular season games. I love the fluidity of it, sprinting down the sidelines, gauging the ball floating high over my shoulder, the subtle adjustment of direction, the feel of the ball lightly touching down upon my fingertips. Catching a football is where I have always felt most at home, most competent in the world. But of course chuckball isn't an official seminary sport, so it's hard to get a game organized.

Spring blooms and we start hardball season. I'm playing first base, Al Potter's squatting behind the plate, giving signs to Pat Browne on the mound. Pat's not looking at Al's signs or at the batter. He's looking down at his shadow, checking his form as he goes into the windup. He nails the first batter in the butt with a fastball. The second guy hits a grounder through the shortstop. Potts calls time-out, comes out to the mound. I head over from first base in case they want to try to pick the runner off. Potts' face is flushed, ringed in dusty sweat as he pulls off his mask. "Watch the goddamn signals, will you? That was supposed to be a curveball." Pat kicks the rubber with his spikes. "Screw you, Potts. He just got lucky. It should have been an out."

In the last game I catch a spike on the ankle when Pat tries to pick off a runner at first. It bruises up pretty badly, but there are no bright red spots as there used to be. The blood disease seems to be fading away. Good thing, since it's the end of the year and I still haven't told my folks I'm playing sports.

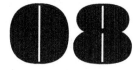

---

## AW HELL!

---

The year winds down and the Indians come in last again after a poor performance in the swim meet. Our only victory is Al Potter's second place in the plunge, a strange event requiring only buoyancy and breath. The entire student body gathers around the pool for the final awards ceremony and watches as the green flag of the Ramblers is run up on the flagpole, followed by the Trojan red, the Bear blue, and the Indian yellow. Disgusted I leave before the ceremony is over.

Tom Sheehan and Ed Gaffney win most of our class's academic premiums and Father Campbell announces next year's house job assignments, keyboy, student store, librarian, master of ceremonies, sacristan, infirmarian. I don't get picked for a job, probably because I'm a non-orig. The next day is a bustle of packing. I empty my locker into a laundry bag and watch McLaughlin push stiff socks and sweat-stained BOs into a cardboard box atop cleats and mitt. The voices are louder than usual, more excited, and touched slightly with anxiety. Summer vacation is more than a break; it is also a test. During the summer some will decide not to return to the seminary; perhaps they have already decided. I look around the locker room, search the faces for any hint of finality.

The next morning cars begin to arrive, parking around the building, jockeying for places near the stairs. I spot our green Chevy sitting in the same place it was when I moved in, nine months ago. My dad is in the driver's seat smoking his pipe. "Hi Darlin'," he gets out of the car as I walk up. "All packed?" He gives me a kiss on top of my head and takes the top box out of my arms. "Your mother's teaching, so I get you all to myself." He sets the load in the back seat and grins at me as we head back up the stairs together for the rest of my stuff. "You made it," he tells me. I nod and grin back. "Have I told you how proud I am of you, Darlin'?" he asks.

"Hmm," I say. "Let's see … only about a million times." He laughs and pats me on the back. "Well then, one more time won't hurt."

We carry the chest of drawers down to a storeroom, and manage the rest of the stuff in three trips. Guys are shouting "Have a good summer" to each other as they pass on the steps. I stick my head in Frank Healy's room to say goodbye. He hesitates, then says, "Yeah, maybe I'll see you in Marin." He flashes a quizzical little smile. I'll recall that smile when I return the next Fall and he's not there.

"You still remember how to drive, Darlin'?" My dad hands me the keys. He goes around to the passenger side and I slide behind the wheel. I drive down the lane to St. Joseph's Avenue, turn left on Grant Road. "Wow, the car is steering a lot easier," I say. My dad smiles. "I had to install power steering because my arm's been giving me a little trouble." He rubs his right shoulder. I feel my stomach tighten and glance at him, he looks thinner somehow at the neck and cheeks. His hair is a lighter shade of grey. "How's retirement treating you?" I ask him. "Goin' on two years," he says. "Not bad, not bad," he reaches down, pulls his right leg up, and shifts in his seat. "The real estate stuff keeps me going. But I'm 72, an old codger. I can't compete with these young puppies," he reaches over and tousles my hair. He used to seem ageless, but now as he sits there, worrying the crease of his right pants leg with his long tapered fingers, he looks a little fragile, breakable. "Your mother laughs at me because I always make friends with my customers. Hell," he laughs, glancing over at me, "half the time I talk them out of buying the house because I don't think they can afford it. She says I should have been a social worker."

We turn into Inman Avenue and the big elm across the street welcomes me home. I return to my job with the maintenance crew at Marin Catholic and answer their many questions about seminary life. My dad's real estate office is in Kentfield, so I often stop on my way home from work to visit with him and his partner, Al Kelly. They're usually sitting at their desks reading the paper or talking. Al's an old friend from St. Anselm's parish, one of those who dutifully contributed to my drab seminary wardrobe the summer before. He often teases me about the ties.

I'm writing a letter at the kitchen table on a hot Saturday afternoon when the phone rings. My mother sets down the flowers she's arranging, wipes her hands on her apron, and picks it up. "Oh hi, Al." I watch her smile dim as she listens. "Yes, Al, I would appreciate that very much. Greg can get the car later."

She hangs up the phone, takes a deep breath. "Al says there's something wrong with your dad. He's acting dizzy and disoriented. He's going to drive him home."

I'm watching out the living room window as Al drives up. He goes around and opens my dad's door, helps him walk shakily to the front of the house. My mother is already down the stairs, grabbing Dad's other arm, and I follow her. "Joe, dear, are you all right?"

"Fine, Darlin'. I'm just … just … "

We get him up the stairs, into an easy chair in the living room. I pull the hassock closer to the chair and sit down in front of him. "How's it going, Dad?" He has a far-off look in his eyes and he doesn't seem to be able to focus on me. I hear my mother in the kitchen talking to the doctor. "Right away," she says.

"I'm … " my father says. "I have … " he starts again. "There … " He puts his fingers to his forehead, squints at me forcing a smile. He can't seem to put his words together. They keep fading off.

The ambulance takes my dad to St. Joseph's in San Francisco, where I was born, where my mother will feel safe. "I want you to stay home," she tells me. "Help Grandad get dinner." I stand on the front steps with my grandfather, watching her get into Mrs. Pulskamp's big Buick and drive off toward the hospital.

I'm lying in bed reading an Evelyn Waugh novel from my mother's Catholic book club when the car pulls up and I hear her say thanks and close the car door. A minute later she appears in my doorway, braced against the door jam as she takes a deep breath. "He's resting," she says. "Tomorrow they're going to do some tests, inject some dye into his bloodstream and see if it gets blocked anywhere."

"Is he going to be okay?" I ask.

"I hope so," she looks past me, out the dark window into the night. "We just need to remember him in our prayers."

My mother goes back the next morning, returns in time to make dinner. I come up from the basement, ease into a chair across from my grandfather. She picks up a potato and begins peeling it slowly, letting the long peels roll into the sink. "It's a stroke," she says wearily. "A blockage on the left side of the brain, which impairs his speech and affects the muscles on the right side of the body."

"Will he get better?" I want her to come over and take my face in her cool wet hands, kiss me on the cheek and say, "Oh yes, everything's going to be fine." I want that image of my dad stumbling on his words to disappear.

My mother runs the white potato under a stream of water. "The doctors don't know," she says. "We need to pray for him."

Two weeks later Mrs. Pulskamp's Buick rolls into our driveway. I can see my dad's slumped form in the passenger's seat, and I run out the front door. When he turns to look at me through the glass, his sweet smile is twisted down on the right side into a frozen pucker. I open the door while my mother and Mrs. Pulskamp come around to help me. "Hey, Dad," I say. I lift his knees up and swing his legs out of the car. He puts his left arm around my shoulders and I pull him to a standing position. "I ... I ... I ... " he tries, and then says, "Aw Hell!" I look over at my mother and she shakes her head. When I look back at him, his eyes have the look of someone whose wallet has just been stolen. We steady him as he crosses the front walk, methodically moving his left foot then dragging the right around to meet it. We boost him one stair at a time and let him rest at the top, before continuing through the living room to his bedroom.

Easing him down on his bed, I take off his shoes and my mother empties his toiletry kit into the medicine chest. He closes his eyes and I pull an afghan up around his shoulders. "I'm going to let you rest a while," I tell him. "Mmm," he says.

Sitting at the kitchen table, my mother rotates her wedding ring as she stares down at the pile of hospital forms in front of her. When she looks up, her eyes are filled with tears. "It's going to be okay, Momma." I sit down across from her. "He's going to get better."

"No," she says sadly, "I don't think so. I think I've lost my Joe."

I don't believe her. I can't imagine such a thing.

The rest of the summer, still nattily attired in his slacks and oxfords, my dad sits in his favorite stuffed chair. He turns the pages of the *Saturday Evening Post*. But his gaze is vacant. He forgets to put on his reading glasses. Occasionally he tries to say something, hits an invisible wall, backs up and takes another run at it, until finally he gives up in frustration.

My mother signs up for driving lessons, jokes about being the oldest student in the class, prepares for an unknown future. I deny the finality of it, pray for his full recovery and find myself spending long hours lying in bed, unable to sleep, looking forward to softball season at the seminary.

## NEAR DEATH EXPERIENCE

1958, my second year of seminary is a banner year for vocations. The seminary is so crowded the sixth-Latiners double up and our class is moved to the new college wing. The year is punctuated by three things: the Pope's death, the liturgical movement, and my appendix.

The only Pope I've ever known is Pope Pius XII, who's been in office almost 20 years, and we're allowed to watch the news the night he dies. I'm surprised to hear the commentators speculating about his possible successors. How can newscasters think they can second-guess the Holy Spirit? The next few weeks the faculty floods us with news clippings about cardinals converging on Rome. We gather around the radio in the rec room when the voting starts, hoping to hear that white smoke is coming out of St. Peter's. We're surprised when it keeps coming out black.

Visiting Sundays, my parents and Grandad still come. My father listens docilely as I tell him funny stories about my classmates and teachers. Too eagerly I take his laughter for comprehension. My mother and I walk together around the seminary grounds. "He's still such a dear," she says, "but he's not the Joe I knew. That person is gone."

I don't know how to respond to her grief, so I switch to my seminary persona, say something about accepting God's will. She stops and looks at me, her narrowed eyes and the strain in her neck are the marks of irritation. I know this because in younger years she would look like this before she called me by my full name and told me to stay away from that dirty old creek or quit tracking mud into the house. Then she does an unexpected thing, she reaches over and hugs me, I smell her faint perfume and I know she is consoling me for understanding so little.

On the morning of the 28th, three days after the voting for a new Pope starts, we walk into Latin class and see scribbled on the blackboard: "First Irish Pope – Ron Kelly." I don't get the joke until Father Campbell comes in and announces that Cardinal Roncalli has just been elected Pope John XXIII. After class, Ed Gaffney's stentorian voice rings out: "Roncalli's a compromise candidate. He's old and they figure he'll die in a couple of years. That'll give the liberals and conservatives time to line up their votes." Liberals and conservatives? What's he talking about? Aren't the cardinals all inspired by the Holy Spirit?

The new pope surprises everyone by convening an ecumenical council. Suddenly change is in the air. Ed and other guys talk about something called the *liturgical movement.* They carry around *Worship Magazine,* books by Pius Parsch and Godfrey Diekmann. They want the Mass translated into the vernacular. They want to wear long surplices with swooping necklines instead of the traditional square-cut ones. They want everyone to have Bible stands in their rooms and read the scriptures half an hour a day. The jocks call them *Movers* and make fun of them. "Hey Gaff, how's your movement today?" I try reading a Pius Parsch book, but it's all flapdoodle to me. I'm disgusted when Bob Murnane, the rebel hero of our eighth grade class, becomes a Mover and says we should get together and recite Vespers every day during our vacation. Good God! Rattling off a bunch of psalms is about as inspiring as a toothache. What's happened to these guys? The Movers start a weekly art forum, trying to make up for what they consider the woeful lack of seminary aesthetics. Pat Browne raises an eyebrow. "Yeah, they just want to check out the dirty pictures in those art books."

My confessor, Father Perkowski, gets reassigned to another seminary. Rather than choosing one of the popular confessors I pick the scariest guy on the faculty. Tall and broad-shouldered with a severely chiseled face and an unruly mane of grey hair, Father Charlie Dillon is nicknamed Zeus, stemming from his habit of hooking his index finger at us as if he's shooting lightning bolts.

When I confess to Father Dillon that I don't find bible reading and liturgical study very inspiring, he lets out a guffaw. "Don't be stupid. All those fancy new movements are for eggheads. Just stick to The Imitation of Christ."

Spy Wednesday, my second Easter season at the seminary. This is the day Judas agreed to hand Jesus over to the Sanhedrin for 30 pieces of silver. I kneel in chapel for night prayers and I think how disappointed Jesus must have been when Judas came up and kissed him in the garden. I feel a strange pain in my stomach, but it's trivial compared to Jesus' pain, which was so bad his sweat came out as drops of blood.

I wake up in the middle of the night, nauseous and sweating, clutching my abdomen. I think again of Jesus and unite my pain with his, half glad for this opportunity to suffer with him. Doubled over, I make my way down the darkened corridor to the bathroom. The vomiting relieves the nausea, but it intensifies the pain. By the time I get back to my room I'm dizzy. I collapse on my bed in the fetal position, suspecting now that something is wrong, praying I can bear it.

In the morning, I ignore the bell, and lie in bed, listening to slippers shuffling down to the bathroom and back, water running, toothbrushes being rapped on washbasins. Doors close, footsteps hurry past my door, and resound down the hollow staircase. Silence again.

I wait until I'm sure everyone's gone to chapel, then slowly stand and cinch my bathrobe. The infirmary is at the opposite end of the building two floors up. I trudge down the front corridor, gagging as I pass Beansy's cigar-scented room, and turn down a hallway of silent student rooms toward the far staircase. I climb one step at a time, stop often to catch my breath, wipe the sweat from my forehead, ask Jesus for help, feeling close to him.

Mrs. Doherty is shaking down a thermometer when I push open the door. A first-high kid is sitting up in one of the beds, pajamas and hair still rumpled from sleep.

"Well, what can we do for you this morning?" she says in her creaky voice. "Did Father Fausel send you up?"

Clammy and nauseous, I sink into the hard wooden chair next to the door. "No."

"Well you know you need permission to come up here, either from Father or from one of the infirmarians."

"Sorry, I think I'm going to throw up." I cup my hand over my mouth and reach for the wastebasket.

All day I lie on the white bed, barely aware of the sounds around me, blood throbbing in my ears as I sweat through the sheets. Nurse Doherty takes the thermometer out of my mouth and frowns. "Higher still," she says. "Are you sure you won't let me give you an enema?" I shake my head, remembering my mother's mantra about never taking an enema when your stomach hurts.

When I wake up again, the afternoon shadows are longer, and I'm shivering under wet sheets. "You're still awfully hot," Mrs. Doherty says, straightening the soggy bedclothes. "Father Fausel wants to call your parents. He thinks you better go home." The student infirmarians arrive with dinner trays. I wave them off and sink back into woozy sleep. When I wake up, it is to the sound of my dad's voice, "Darlin', I … you … go home." I see Mrs. Pulskamp across the room talking quietly to Mrs. Doherty.

Mrs. Pulskamp guides me a step at a time toward the elevator. My dad walks ahead of us, dragging his right leg. He uses his left arm to hold the elevator door open for us. Downstairs we come out into cool twilight. There are blankets spread across the back seat of Mrs. Pulskamp's

Buick. I settle onto them.

"Comfy, Darlin'?"

My response seems far away.

The car doors open and I hear my mother's voice. "Thanks again, Frances. I don't know what we would have done without you." My mother puts a cool hand to my cheek. "Can you stand up, dear?" Very carefully, I push myself out of the car and hobble toward the front stairs. Once I reach my room I collapse onto the high bed. Next I know, Dr. Russell's tanned face is smiling down at me. "I'm going to feel around a little," he says, touching my stomach. A moment later, he pulls the stethoscope from his ears. "Let's get an ambulance here right away."

Relaxing into the gurney, I imagine the attendants are Roman soldiers, carrying me to the scourging post.

Blurred voices, the drone of a machine. I try to open my eyes. My lids rise, then fall shut again. I force them back open, see bleary images of tubes running from plastic bags, dials and meters, my mother's face, leaning in close. "Hi, dear."

"What happened, Momma?" Her hair is matted down on one side, her eyes are shrouded in dark circles. "The doctor had to take out your appendix. It ruptured and got infected." Tears cloud her eyes. "Why did you wait so long to call us?"

*So long?* I fade back into a dream of Nurse Doherty with her thermometer, Jesus sweating blood. When I awaken again, my mother's hair is neatly combed and she's wearing a new blouse. The dark circles are still there.

"Everyone's praying for you," she whispers. All the kids at Marin Catholic and all your friends in the seminary." She adjusts the sheets and I drift back to sleep, savoring the tears people will be shedding at my funeral.

I feel a hand on my forehead and open my eyes. My mom and dad are standing by my bed, smiling. "Good news," my mother says. "The doctor just took you off the critical list. You're going to be okay." My dad wraps his fingers around my hand, squeezes. "The Blessed Mother must have heard our prayers," my mom continues. "We asked for a miracle and we got one. The operation was Holy Thursday and you stayed on the critical list all through Good Friday and Holy Saturday. Do you know what day today is?" I don't.

"Easter Sunday. We got our resurrection, thank God." I know I should share their joy, but what about dying young and leaving a beautiful memory? What about the glory of martyrdom? What about going to the grave with Jesus? I look at the massive bandage taped across my stomach. Now I have to haul my wimp ass back to the seminary and start all over.

# 10

## APOLOGETICS, RHETORIC, FOOTBALL

It's not as bad as I thought. The six-inch scar heals quickly and by the end of May I'm playing baseball again. That summer I get a job at the CYO day camp in San Rafael. Other classmates work at residential camps near the Russian River, and I'd like to join them, but I don't want to be away from my dad that much. Our time together has gotten more precious to us both.

In the fall we start college as Poets. Next year we'll be called Rhets. Things feel very different. Several of our old classmates have dropped out and lots of new guys, including Jim Pulskamp, have transferred in from various high schools. "You'll like Jim," I tell my friends. "He's really funny." But Jim comes in shy and serious. I wish he'd cut loose and be his funny self.

We have Father O'Neill for Apologetics class. He's the most colorful character on the faculty, famous for his absent-mindedness. One morning he comes out of the professor's dining room and stops John Cunningham in the cloister. "Son, did you see where I just came from?"

"Yes, Father, the dining room."

"Oh good. I must have eaten breakfast."

We call him Johnny O, though sometimes I hear guys call him "Beak" because of his big curved nose. When he talks in class, he squints his eyes and looks over his nose like he's sighting a rifle. We sit at our desks, waiting for Johnny O to come and teach us how to defend our faith against heretics, atheists, and secular humanists. He's always late for class, probably because he can never remember where he's going. Finally he charges in with a huge armload of books and papers and throws them on the desk. Then he sits down and glares up at the water pipe running across the ceiling. We wait until he settles down and remembers where he is. He reaches for the Apologetics book, opens it to a marker, and reads a paragraph. He frowns and stares up at the pipe again. "Gentleman, people are always criticizing the Inquisition, but the Inquisition was the best thing the heretic ever knew! Good God, if you're doomed to Hell you should be grateful that somebody's willing to torture you out of it." We sit in silence. He often goes on rants like this. It's part of his Irish bellicosity. He's on the front line of the battle against Satan.

I'm impressed by Johnny O's certainty, despite his obvious eccentricities. He's a fanatic, but so am I. We are solitary warriors, fighting the good fight against trivia and compromise. Most of my classmates seem to be just sliding along, playing both sides of the priest coin, unwilling to live up to Jesus' demands. I alone can heed the call. I alone can deny myself the luxuries of comfort and compromise. I alone am called to true sacrifice. (I am a real pain in the ass.)

The biggest change this year is the college sports system. Instead of being a Rambler or an Indian, you get picked on a different team for every sport. And since it's no longer mandatory, a lot of guys don't play anymore. They just walk around and talk.

Softball season I end up playing on the same team as McLaughlin. "This is weird, isn't it?" I say as we run out on the field together. He doesn't say anything, just heads out to shortstop and starts scratching the dirt with his spikes. Pat Browne's playing first base on the other team. When I get up to bat, he starts yelling, "Right field hitter. Shift right." He knows all my secrets.

Chemistry's the toughest class we have. Father Dillon stands at the blackboard furiously writing formulas with one hand and erasing them with the other. Students who are smart in everything else are surprised when they start getting "C"s in Chemistry. And other guys, like Ozzie Hoffman and Maurice Maybury, suddenly emerge as geniuses. I eke out a "B," but I don't feel as if I really understand any of it.

The Movers grow more bold, flaunting their plunging necklines and brightly-colored vestments before the glowering traditionalists. Al Larkin and Gerry Winkenbach have been working down in the craft room for weeks, pasting mosaic tiles on a five-foot high cone that will replace the old paschal candle stand. On Easter Saturday they unveil the thing in the chapel, and I hear the jocks snuffling in the pews. "It looks like a nose cone from NASA," McLaughlin whispers to MacNamara. He puts his hand over his mouth like a walkie-talkie. "Ground control to Winky, ready for launch."

In Apologetics, Johnny O is critiquing all the philosophers who diverged from Thomas Aquinas. "What do you know about Immanual Kant?" he thunders. Someone says, "Phenomenon and noumenon.."

"No!" Johnny O cuts him off. "That man had boxes in his head! He couldn't tell the difference between ideas and real life. What does he do when he gets a parking ticket, tell the judge it's just an idea?"

Next we cover the Protestant Reformation. "What do you need to remember about Martin Luther?" Johnny O asks. Hands go up. "He was against indulgences," one says. "He wrote the ninety-five theses," another says. "And tacked them on the door of the cathedral," adds someone else.

"No!" Johnny O yells at the water pipe. "He was a horny monk who ended up marrying a nun. That's all you need to know about Mr. Luther."

For the last class, he comes in with a huge stack of tests, drops them on the desk and addresses the water pipe. "All right. There will be no talking during this test, no questions asked, no questions answered. When you finish, bring up your test and leave the room in silence." He passes out the tests without making eye contact, then sits down and picks up his breviary. We look at the tests. A hand goes up, then another. He glances up, glares up at the pipe again. "I said no questions asked, no questions answered." Back to reading his breviary. We sit in obedient, strained silence for ten minutes. Cunningham lets out a "B'sht" cough. Everyone bursts into laughter. Johnny O'Neill jumps out of his chair.

"All right. What's so funny?"

"Father, you teach us Apologetics. This is a Greek test."

My confessor, Father Dillon, teaches Rhetoric that year, and we have to get up in front of the class and give speeches. He's brutal. "McAllister, that speech was totally sophomoric." I turn red, blistering at his attack. "Do you know what that word means?"

"No," I say, "like a sophomore?"

"Like somebody who doesn't know what he's talking about. Somebody who's spouting out opinions with no substantiation."

Man! My own confessor is beating me up in public. I go to the chapel that night and talk it over with Jesus. Back in my room, I write carefully in my new journal.

*My first speech this year was a real masterpiece, I thought. It was my own original opinion, and I expected it to be greeted with enthusiasm and applause. Instead, Fr. Dillon said it was just opinion without substantiation. At this my pride flared and I was disgusted with myself for allowing myself to be humiliated. I should have been thankful for God's warning against pride.*

I just finished reading St. Theresa's autobiography. I'm hoping someone will stumble on this journal after my death, read my words, and maybe propose me for canonization.

Jim Pulskamp stands in front of Dillon's class for his first speech. His hair is neatly combed, his sash adjusted tightly around his cassock. "What I did this summer." He breathes in and looks out at us, his eyes wide, a slight smile playing around his lips. "Well," he says, "this summer, I worked in a judge's office. And I had the very important job of greasing law books with neats-foot oil." He raises his bushy eyebrows at us and folds his lips. "Now, I'm not altogether sure what a neat is." His face morphs into a frown, "But I assume it's an animal with very big feet." Everyone laughs. He rolls his eyes and they laugh again. They keep laughing all the way through his speech.

The next time he stands up to give a speech, all he has to do is look at us and we start laughing. Father Dillon says, "Pulskamp, can't you give a serious speech?" Jim nods and stares down at the floor for a minute, collecting his thoughts. His face is serious when he starts again, but then a faint lift of his eyebrow sends us into hysterics. The harder he tries to be serious, the more we laugh. Finally Father Dillon threatens to flunk him if he can't give a serious speech. Fearing for his survival, we keep our eyes down and make it through the speech without laughing. Now everyone knows I wasn't kidding. Jim is a very funny guy.

In early October Tom Sheehan, our class president, calls a meeting in the Rhet classroom after lunch. "It seems we have a challenge to meet," he says and nods to Mike Murray. Mike stands up, leans back against his desk and folds his arms. "As you may know, it's traditional every fall for the First Philosophers at St. Pat's to challenge the Rhets to a touch football game. We have about a month to get ready, so I've scheduled our first practice for next

Tuesday. It's six-man touch, so we'll need at least a dozen guys on the team. Purcell's going to send me the rules this week, so I'll get them to you by Tuesday."

There's no doubt in anyone's mind that Mike should lead the team. He's the best strategist in the class, very smart in math, the former captain of the Bears. I think back on one of our soccer games in fourth high. We were right in front of the Bear's goal, about to score, and Mike, realizing there was no other way to prevent it, picked up the ball and threw it out of bounds. The ref didn't see it, and they went on to win the game. I was furious at the time, but now I'm glad to have Mike leading our team.

On Tuesday afternoon everyone's a little nervous as we suit up in the locker room. None of us have ever played football together. We have no idea who's going to make the team. Even McLaughlin seems preoccupied as he laces up his cleats. Brady and MacNamara are more quiet than usual, smiling as Pat Browne does an exaggerated imitation of a sportscaster. "Minutes to go in the half. Poly up by seven. Nevin flanks wide for St. Ignatius. The snap, the quarterback steps back to throw, lets it go long, down the right side. Nevin's there, in the end zone. Touchdown!" Ed Nevin blushes. He's the only one who's played high school football, so the pecking order is shifting in his direction.

Out on the field, Murray goes over the rules. "A tackle is two hands above the waist. No leaving your feet on a block. Only one run every four downs. You have to cross the fifty to get a first down." He breaks us into three groups, ends, halfbacks, linemen. Ed coaches the ends, teaches us the three point stance, how to do a head fake on a defender. Mike works with the quarterbacks and halfbacks, then gets us together for pass patterns. The next practice we start learning basic plays, the button-hook, the stop-go, the in-and-out. By the third practice he announces that Ed and I will start at end.

It's a brisk Thursday morning when we board the bus and head over to St. Pat's. We have no uniforms, just a variety of snarly BOs. McLaughlin, I notice, isn't wearing his cleats, probably because no one else has a pair. Murray's standing in the front of the bus, one hand clutching the pole, the other gesturing plays and strategy. "They'll probably throw to Holland a lot, so we'll double up on him. I'm not sure who their other end will be, maybe Laveroni or Rogers. And I think Purcell's their quarterback." I know all these guys in the class ahead of us, but I've never seen them play football. Purcell's smart, a good basketball player, so I imagine he's a good quarterback. They're probably over at St. Pat's making the same speculations about us. They know Ed was a star at St. Ignatius, so they'll be dogging him for sure.

It's a tight game from the start. They have a few surprises for us, including George Doub, a witty scholar who never played any sports at St. Joe's, but now crashes through the line and nails us twice before we can adjust and put Al Potter between him and the quarterback. On third down, Mike calls a stop-go and points to me. At the snap I take three steps out and spin around. He fakes it to me, drawing Laveroni in to block it. I swivel around and take off down the field looking over my shoulder. I see the ball sailing high toward the left corner. I adjust my stride, angle further left. Leaning forward, stretching my arms out, I feel the ball gently touch down on my fingertips. It's the best feeling in the world. After that Murray and I are unstoppable. We connect for twenty passes, three touchdowns.

After the game everyone is shaking hands. "Good game, man!" They can't hide their surprise as they clap me on the back. I feel great. After four long years, I've carved out a place for myself with these guys. I'm no longer a wimp.

# 11

## TRANSITION SUMMER

The round little tailor dances around me, measuring front and back with his tape. His wide smile is suspended like a bridge between two shiny pear cheeks. Remnants of black serge litter the floor in the tiny shop, cutting shears and patterns lie atop a long table. It's May 1961, just before my graduation from St. Joseph's – a mongrel graduation, neither high school nor college, since the minor seminary spans six years. I'm about to begin another six years at St. Patrick's major seminary and this will require a costume change. Rather than drab ties and jackets, we'll be required to wear cassocks every day, shrouding ourselves in the black cloth of self-immolation from dawn to dusk. The best and priciest cassocks are those hand-crafted by Pete Thyssen, this jolly Dutchman whose father and grandfather also specialized in clerical garb. Less expensive models can be purchased from Cabrini Church Supplies in San Francisco, but these tend to develop a greenish sheen after a few months – *Cabrini Greenies*. The only other option is mail order from Hong Kong, but you can never be sure the cassock will fit when it arrives. Since I have no doubts about my priestly vocation, I decide to invest in a high-end Thyssen cassock, hoping it will last me the full six years. Pete jots down a final measurement, grins, and tells me when to come back for a final fitting.

Summer arrives and twice a week I drive over to Bob Carroll's house in San Francisco to edit the film we shot last semester at St. Joe's. We're anxious to get it finished so we can show it as soon as we get to St. Pat's. I drive through the Sunset district to an upscale neighborhood whose stucco houses always seem bleak to me, even without the pervasive fog. Narrow strips of grass interrupt the pervasive asphalt like afterthoughts. Bob opens the door and welcomes me into an elegant living room. His mother comes out of the kitchen wiping freckled hands on a frilly apron. "Greg, it's good to see you. We'll have dinner in just a little bit. Bobbie, where are your manners, take his jacket." She has a Gracie Allen zaniness that Bob likes to fuel with hyperbole and satire. His father retreats to his study, away from the line of fire. After dinner Bob and I excuse ourselves and go down to the basement where a card table holds several film canisters and a small editing machine. We scrape emulsion off tiny ends of 8 mm film, apply glue, press them together and review the scene by rolling the new splice through the viewer. It's tedious work and too often the splice breaks, but the excitement of premiering our movie at the seminary keeps us going. Bob has decided to call the film *The Sweet Life*, a takeoff on *La Dolce Vita*, recently condemned by the Legion of Decency. As scenes roll through the viewer, I realize that Bob has been visualizing Fellini and Truffaut while I was thinking Laurel and Hardy. The result is a noir slapstick about an alienated loner who attempts to survive an oppressive, often ridiculous, seminary regimen. Bob holds a small microphone to the phonograph's latticed speaker as I lower the needle onto tracks from The Everly Brothers, Petula Clark, and honky tonk piano riffs from Knuckles O'Toole. We try to synchronize the sound track with the film, but it never comes out right.

At St. Pat's that fall, we show the movie to about thirty seminarians in a dingy basement room. Bob runs the projector and I run the Wollensak recorder and each of us periodically stops to let the other catch up. Our audience laughs at the slapstick, but misses the deeper symbolism, which is a relief to me, since I didn't get it either. Bob doesn't care. He knows a few people will get it.

# 12

---

## SEEDS OF DISSENT

---

My new confessor at St. Pat's is Father William Sheehy, a gentle and saintly octogenarian. He hears my confessions for two months then gets sick and dies. I shop around for someone else, finally opting for the faculty equivalent of George Patton. Father Red Cronan is an ex-military chaplain with a Ph.D. in Psychology. He teaches us philosophy from a textbook written in Latin, pacing back and forth like a master sergeant, barking syllogisms and honing Thomistic distinctions like bayonets, preparing us for our war against secular humanists and fuzzy liberals.

That Friday night I stand outside Red's door waiting my turn for confession. The odor of stale cigarette smoke permeates the hallway. I hear an upper classman, Charlie Benken laugh and say "Thanks, Father" as he opens the door and walks past me. I enter and kneel on the *prei dieu* next to Red's chair. He's wearing a thin stole around his neck, resting his chin on nicotine stained fingers. His coppery hair is combed straight back, framing a rugged James Cagney face. "Bless me Father, it's been one week since my last confession." When I finish my list of feeble sins he gives me my penance and rattles off the Latin absolution in a gravelly voice. Then, breaking the ice, he asks me how my summer went. "Fine," I say.

"Don't kid yourself, Mac, it's a battle. The world on one side … " He holds up his clenched left fist, then punches out his right, "God on the other. Matter versus spirit." He draws both fists together. "You have to keep your guard up." I'm distracted by his yellowed fingertips, what they say about his own battle with the world. But I like his gruff style and the fact that most of my classmates are terrified of him. Even a faint approval from Red will be a coup.

After about a week it's clear that the fuzzy liberal Red is always berating is our other philosophy professor, Father Giguere. Nicknamed "Cheech," Giguere is diminutive. He looks like a scared chipmunk, but his probing intellect and openness to new ideas stand in stark contrast to Red's macho sophistry and eventually infect even the most cynical and hard-headed of us. From him we learn about existential doubt, the glory of angst, the shallowness of traditional Thomism.

Father Lyman Fenn in Theology is on Red's side. His grey hair is always meticulously combed and his cassock spotless. He's Bing Crosby in *Going My Way*. Smiling benevolently during his moral theology class, he skewers the liberals as "joy boys of the Resurrection." "Remember, gentlemen, love without law is the height of folly."

We file into the spiritual reading hall one night and notice a well-dressed gentleman standing next to Father Wagner on the front dais. "Who's that?" McLaughlin whispers as we're sitting down on the hard slat-back chairs. I shrug my shoulders. Father Wagner looks out at the assembly, waiting for several faculty members to find seats. "We have a special guest this evening. Mr. Sam Allen here is a parishioner at St. Raymond's and a therapist at the VA Hospital in Palo Alto. He has asked to share some information with you." Allen stands, straightens his tie and smiles. "You probably know that alcoholism is a big problem for our vets. It's very hard to cure and the recidivism rate is very high." Several seminarians nod their heads. "Lately, though, we've been experimenting with a new drug that's showing incredible results. Patients who take it seem to lose their craving for alcohol completely. Tests have shown that it releases a rare chemical in the brain that is found only among monks who have spent years in contemplation. That's why I thought you gentlemen would be interested in hearing about it. It seems to bridge the gap between body and soul." There is a moment of stunned silence, then the new Philosophy teacher raises his hand. "Yes, Father?" Allen says.

"I would personally like to volunteer as a test subject for your program."

"That would be wonderful," says Allen. "We're always looking for … "

Father Fenn's voice booms from the back of the hall. "This is against the natural law. It should be condemned!"

It isn't long before the U.S. Government does condemn LSD.

The Vatican Council is about to start and it's clear that the Catholic Church is no longer a monolithic institution.

Huge battles are being waged over such topics as religious liberty, Church governance, and birth control. Father Frank Norris teaches dogmatic theology at St. Pat's and has recently published a book about the early Church. We're excited when he gets invited to attend the Council as a *peritus* (expert) during the drafting of the Constitution on the Church. At Mass the next Sunday, he gives the sermon. He comes out in a new silk vestment, colorful and flowing. His face is round, his cheeks shiny, almost cherubic, and he speaks in a pedantic voice, chewing his words like an expensive steak. "*Ecclesia*, the people of God!" he begins. I see Lyman Fenn's painted-on smile fade as he glares down at the floor. "The real Church is not some authoritarian structure based on the Roman Empire, but a collegial body united in brotherly love." Several of the older faculty squirm uncomfortably in their seats. Frank is sticking it to them. The next week it's Fenn's turn to preach. He comes to the pulpit in a stiff square chasuble, *fiddlebacks* they're called. I remember as a kid when I served Mass and had to grab the back and hold it up during the consecration. It always felt like cardboard. Lyman makes the sign of the cross, then reads a passage from the day's liturgy. He looks up at us and his sweet singsong voice cloaks his words in benevolence, mesmerizing us so that we're unprepared when he slips in his barbs. "Sometimes we forget that the Church is not a democracy. As priests we are not called to freedom, but to obedience to the will of God. There is no modernizing the Gospel. We've had schisms in the Church before. Let us pray we don't have one again."

I'm confused. I sit in my pew in chapel and look over at the faculty. How can these scholarly men of God be contradicting each other? I look at them again, more closely, hoping to find someone with Solomon's wisdom. Father Leo Ruskowski has avoided the conflict, and sits impassively among his colleagues, his head tilted back slightly, giving the impression he's amused by the whole debate. His field is Church History, so maybe he has a broader perspective on these issues. But in class he paces robot-like back and forth and speaks in a droning monotone. "History is made up of names and dates." He seems to be fixated on the number three. "Mr. Leger, name three popes between eleven hundred and twelve fifty." Leger lets out a nervous yelp when Leo calls his name. His face turns bright red and his eyes glaze over, like he's about to vomit. "Uhh, well, um … Innocent the Third and … maybe Gregory the Ninth? And uh … Innocent the Fourth?" Leo continues his catatonic pace. "Name three more."

Later I'm told by an upper classman that Father Ruskowski was an early recipient of a prefrontal lobotomy, which left him fixated on the trinity. Legend has it that they sawed a round hole in the top of his head to perform the operation. Hence his nickname, *Cookie Jar.*

The only non-Catholic on the faculty is Doctor Edward Philpot Mumford, an Anglican. He studied entomology at Oxford and subsequently discovered a rare beetle, now known as the Mumford Beetle. He teaches us Biology in an old dark-paneled classroom that opens into a musty lab with stained beakers, pickled frogs, and an anatomical dummy missing its genitals. The Doctor has wispy grey curls and a wattle that vibrates as he reads his notes at us. He appoints John Cunningham to run the projector for the instructional films. Every time the Doctor turns his back, John reverses the projector and we watch young fish swimming backward into egg sacks. We constantly needle the gullible Doctor about the dummy. "Doctor, our dummy doesn't seem to have any reproductive organs. Is that some kind of evolutionary anomaly?"

"Aaaa," sighs the Doctor, glancing nervously over his tortoise-shell glasses, "Father Wagner has asked me not to cover evolution in this class." We all groan our feigned disappointment.

Five years later we will discover what happened to the missing genitals. In our last year in the seminary, just after we have taken the oath of celibacy, we will study a tract in Moral Theology entitled *De Sexu*. Here, for the first time, sexuality will be discussed. Father Fenn will arrive at class that day carrying a brown paper bag. He will reach inside the bag and pull out the genitals purloined from our hapless biology dummy. These will serve as props for his lecture on the morality of sex. Very few will remember the words of that lecture. Everyone will remember the props.

The Vatican Council starts in 1962 and Red Cronan is now teaching us the History of Philosophy. He assigns a philosopher to each of us. I get Henri Bergson. Red did his thesis on Bergson, so I'm nervous. But once I start reading <u>The Dual Sources of Morality and Religion</u>, I can't put it down. I sit at my desk, furiously underlining passages and periodically shouting "Yes! That's it!" I'm so excited I have to get up and pace around the room. Up until now I've been schizophrenic about everything – God versus the world, spirit versus matter, good versus evil. For Bergson it's all one, beginning as pure energy, *élan vital*, shooting upward like water in a fountain, then falling back on itself, appearing static, crystallizing into concepts, rules, hierarchies. I begin to see organized religion as a crystallization of the original pure love of Jesus.

Next I read Bergson's book on comedy where he says that laughter is a reaction to the mechanical becoming encrusted on the living. He's so right. All these rules and roles we take so seriously, they're merely encrustations needing to be laughed at. From now on humor will be my spiritual path; the ultimate grace, laughter.

# 15

## MISCHIEF

The annual retreat is not meant to be funny. We spend five days in total silence broken only by the rabid fulminations of the retreat master and the communal prayers which punctuate the day. We are only allowed to talk during the afternoon softball games, but even there we're encouraged to keep a contemplative attitude. The last day of the retreat I sit at my desk reading a devotional passage from <u>The Major Seminarian</u>. My mind begins to wander and my back tingles with nervous energy. Not much longer, just a few more hours and this retreat will be over. I get up, walk around the room trying to remember what I was reading. Something draws me to the closet. I take out a wire coat hanger, unwind it. Using the curly end as an augur, I begin drilling through the plaster wall that separates my room from Bob Leger's. The hanger crunches its way through the first layer of plaster, then pops through hollow space until it hits the other side. I feel the hanger chewing through another layer of plaster, then breaking through again, only to hit another obstacle. What could that be? I pull out the hanger, straighten it, and re-insert it. Pushing hard, I feel the obstacle slowly give way, followed by a loud crash in

Leger's room. I pull back my hanger and listen. No other sounds. Bob must be in the chapel. I return to my desk suppressing a fierce internal laugh.

Fifteen minutes later Bob returns to his room. He yelps when he opens his door. The contents of his overturned bookcase are scattered all over the floor. That night the retreat officially ends at dinner and five days of silence explode into a crescendo of chatter. I look over at Bob's table and see him talking and gesturing. His tablemates are laughing and now he points over at me. After dinner he leaves the group he's walking with and comes over to Pat Browne and me. "All right, McAllister. When I walked in my room and saw the bookcase turned over and stuff scattered all over the floor, I was baffled. I knew no one would break *The Rule* by crossing the threshold, but I couldn't figure out how it could have happened. Then I saw a little dot of plaster on the back of the bookcase. I estimated where it would have been on the wall and gee, I found a hole drilled from your room. Pretty suspicious."

Pat's laughing. "McAllister's very childish."

"You can say that again." Bob says and bounces off to rejoin his group of friends. Pat shakes his head. "McAllister, why are you always persecuting poor Leger?"

"I'm just trying to enhance his social status." I look over at Bob who seems to be enjoying the re-telling of his story.

Football season has arrived and the new teams are posted on the bulletin board. Pat and I are both on Phil Brady's team along with a couple of good rushers. I've never played on the same team with Phil before. We stand in the huddle and I watch his dark eyes scanning the defense over my shoulder. "Okay, Gregger, down and out to the right. Pat, slant left. On three." Forty-five years later I'll be watching the Patriots in the Super Bowl and see those same eyes scanning the defense – Phil's nephew, Tom. We win every game that season.

Cop Wagner, the seminary rector, comes into the refectory during breakfast one October morning and rings the bell. We all stop talking and look up. He's standing there, slightly stooped, with one hand resting on the faculty dining table. He has a whiny voice. "Last night Archbishop Mitty died in his sleep here at his seminary residence." His eyes sweep the room as though he's looking for an argument. "Please remember him in your prayers." He turns and walks out. We all resume eating. I look over at Len Duggan. He nods his head knowingly. "The Arch has been on waivers for a long time. You want to bet who his successor will be? Five bucks says it's Donohue."

"Jeez, Leonard, the guy just died. Can't you wait until he's buried to start taking odds?"

"How about Merlin Guilfoyle?" says Ed Gaffney. *"When I was one, I'd just begun."* He mimics the auxiliary bishop's nasal voice to recite the poem he's used for the last twenty years at Confirmation ceremonies.

That night I go into the dark chapel and breathe in the aroma of frankincense from yesterday's High Mass. "Eternal rest grant unto him, O Lord, and let perpetual light shine upon him." Does he really need my prayers?

Don't archbishops get automatic passes to Heaven?

Rome remains tight-lipped for four months, while we bet on Mitty's successor. In the meantime, I get a reputation for silly pranks and pride myself as a captain of mischief. Pat Browne, looking superior, calls me immature. I soak him with the enema syringe I've bought in town. "Shit!" he yells and runs away. But no one is a better target than Bob Leger. He's short, very tightly wound, and he actually jumps up in the air when you scare him. In February, when John Glenn prepares to be the first man to orbit the earth, Father Wagner announces at dinner that we have special permission to watch the live coverage that night. At 8 p.m. I sit at my desk listening to the sound of footsteps retreating down the corridor to the TV room. When I'm sure the corridor is empty, I go next door to Bob's room. Very gently I open his door. Careful not to cross the forbidden threshold, I remove the hinge pins and pull the door free. I'm surprised by its weight as I carry it down the hall, past Red Cronan's closed door and into the janitor's closet where I tuck it behind an old mattress. Heart beating, I return to my room, turn off the lights and lie on my bed, laughing quietly in the darkness. Eventually I hear footsteps on the stairs, doors opening and closing. Bob's rapid, hard-heeled footsteps slow as he reaches his doorway, then I hear a deep-throated "Erg!!" followed by muted voices as Bob stops first one, then another, classmate, bewailing his missing door. Suddenly everyone falls silent. I hear the gravelly voice of Red Cronan. "All right, Leger, talk!"

"Er, my door's missing, Father."

"How can you lose a door, Leger?"

Bob's response is gibberish. I feel sorry for him, knowing how terrified he is of Red, but I'm still laughing too hard to do anything. Someone finally locates the door and the next day Bob enjoys even more social prominence. His whole table breaks out laughing as he tells his story at breakfast. Then he turns and shakes his fist at me.

It's February before we hear anything about the new archbishop. Len Duggan sidles up to me on my way to class and whispers, "Today's the day, Mac. They're going to announce the new Arch." Leonard's rumor network, an army of gossip-hungry nuns deployed throughout the Bay Area, is usually reliable. At lunch, Father Wagner stands up and reads the official announcement from the Chancery Office. "The new archbishop of San Francisco is Joseph T. McGuckin, former bishop of Salt Lake City." Everyone starts talking at once. He bangs his palm down on the bell. "Wait," he says, "there's more." When we've quieted down he reads on. "Three new dioceses will be created out of the old San Francisco archdiocese, Oakland, Stockton, and Santa Rosa." I exchange looks with Jim Pulskamp at the next table. Santa Rosa is just north of Marin County. Does that mean Marin will be part of the new diocese? After lunch we take a walk and fantasize about being rural pastors in a diocese that would stretch from the Golden Gate all the way up the coast to Oregon. "That would be great, a little parish in Fortuna or Ukiah." A few days later Father Wagner tells us Marin will remain part of the San

Francisco archdiocese. "Damn!" I say to Jim. "Let's see if we can switch."

The new bishop of Santa Rosa is Leo T. Maher, the former chancellor of the archdiocese. "A financial wizard," Leonard says, "even though he flunked first high Latin. He bought up half of Marin County while he was chancellor."

"How do you know all this stuff, Leonard? Do you have a mole in the Chancery Office?"

Leonard gives me one of his smug grins. "I'll never tell."

A month later we're walking into lunch and I notice Father Wagner escorting two guests up to the faculty table. One is wearing a large gold cross around his neck. "That's him," Leonard whispers. "That's Leo."

"Who's the other guy?" I whisper back.

"Walt Tappe. He used to be the editor of *The Monitor*. Now he's Leo's right-hand man in Santa Rosa." I watch the two of them shaking hands with the faculty, then flanking Father Wagner as he says the grace. Leo has a round, burnished face and the rosy cheeks of an Irish drinker. Tappe is gaunt and angular and clacks a full set of false teeth when he smiles. Father Wagner introduces both of them and then Leo stands, waving to our applause. "It is my great honor," he says, "to have been appointed bishop over a very special tract of land, the beautiful Redwood Empire. I ask your prayers for the success of this undertaking. Thank you." I catch Jim's eye and signal him to meet me after the meal.

"Let's corner Leo and ask him," I say, as we head toward the chapel for the customary post-meal visit. "We'll nab him when he comes out." Leo says a short prayer then genuflects and leaves. Out of deference, everyone else follows his lead. Jim and I are waiting at the door when he emerges. "Excuse us, Bishop, but we'd like to volunteer for your diocese."

He smiles, waits for Tappe to join him. "Some volunteers, Monsignor." He looks back at us. "That's wonderful. You'd certainly be welcome, but of course you'll first have to petition Archbishop McGucken to release you."

"Release us?" I say.

"That's part of canon law," he says looking back at Tappe. "You belong to the bishop whose diocese you reside in. He has to be willing to excardinate you before you can go anywhere else."

"You mean he owns us?" I say. "Like serfs?"

Leo frowns slightly. "That's the way it works. You check with the Archbishop, then we'll talk." He shakes our hands and moves on. As they walk away, I see him wink at Monsignor Tappe. What's that all about?

Len Duggan is sitting in the periodical room reading *National Review.* I sit down across from him and lean in. "Leonard, is it true that you can't switch dioceses without the permission of your bishop?

"Yeah, excardination. Your Ordinary has to agree to release you before you can go anywhere else."

"Isn't that like slavery?"

"Only to radicals like you, Mac. It's canon law. Where have you been?"

"That's crazy."

"Yeah, tell that to the Archbishop."

## LOSS OF FAITH... AND HAIR

In 1959 John Robinson becomes the Anglican bishop of Woolwich, England, and scandalizes the British public by testifying in defense of Lady Chatterly's Lover in a censorship case. Three years later, just after I discover Henri Bergson, Bishop Robinson leans over to tie his shoe and throws out his back. He's immobilized for several weeks and spends the time writing a small book called Honest to God that again sends the British public and the Anglican Church into a frenzy. I buy the book, curious what the fuss is all about. It totally changes my life.

Robinson raises a simple question: If God is "infinite," that is, "without limit or boundary, then how can God be *out there*, separate from ourselves? How can God be a *He*, a distinct person, a Being?

Up until now, I've always spent a lot of time in chapel addressing Jesus in the tabernacle, his small house on the altar. Our communication is enhanced by the aroma of incense, the darkness, the stained glass windows. After reading Honest To God, I still go to the chapel regularly, but instead of talking to Jesus, I just sit there having bizarre arguments with myself:

"Okay, Greg. God is infinite, and Jesus is God, so it's idolatrous for you to be reducing Him to some guy in the tabernacle."

"Yeah, but it's also idolatrous to think he's *not* there."

"But talking implies some kind of subject-object split between you and Him."

"Who you calling *Him*?"

By now my head's spinning. I'm wrestling with finite infinity, contradicting myself at every turn. To liberate God from my mental shackles, I realize, I have to let go of everything I ever believed. And then what's left? Nothing. No thing. God is no thing. Great!

By this time Red Cronan has had a nervous breakdown, so I have a new confessor, Father Nicolas. I tell him about my crisis of faith. He smiles knowingly. "We all have doubts once in a while, Greg. You'll get over it." I talk to other guys who have read Robinson's book, hoping to find comrades in my confusion. "I found it interesting," one says. "I thought the theology was a bit weak," another tells me. What? Don't they get it? Am I going crazy?

Father Mattingly is the shortest priest I've ever seen. He speaks with a slight lisp as he explains to us how God revealed Himself in the scriptures by inspiring the Old and New Testament writers. I listen to him as long as I can, then put my hand up. He points to me, "Yes, Mister McAwester?"

"Father, what exactly do you mean by *God*?"

"Pwease?" he says, looking perplexed. Then he smiles, as though late in getting a joke I just told. He goes back to talking about inspiration.

On Visiting Sunday my mother rides down with the Pulskamps. My dad seldom makes the trip anymore, additional strokes having taken their toll. After chicken and pie with the Pulskamps, my mother and I walk around the grounds. She's more animated than usual. "I just got a new book from the Thomas More book club," she says, pulling a shiny hardback from her bag. "It's a biography of Martin Luther and I'm learning all sorts of things I never knew about him." My mother's been in a Catholic women's book club for years, ever since I was little. A bright and lively bunch, they meet monthly to discuss Graham Greene , Flannery O'Connor and other Catholic writers.

"Does it have an *imprimatur?*"

"Of course" she says with a dismissive flick of her hand. "All the books from Thomas More have to have *imprimaturs.*"

A couple of weeks later the mail boy tosses me a package. I open it and find the book, with a note attached: *I finally finished this. Let me know what you think. -Mom.* I check out the author's bio on the jacket. John Todd, British scholar, convert to Catholicism, conscientious objector in World War II. I begin reading and am immediately captivated by his account of Luther. This isn't the horny monk that Father O'Neill so blithely dismissed in our Apologetics class. This is a sincere churchman whose only crime was to be scandalized by the Vatican selling indulgences to finance the building of St. Peter's. I read on, identifying more and more with Luther, and less and the less with the Catholic Church.

How can my classmates be reading these same books and staying so blase about everything? I feel like a basket case, waking up depressed every morning as though I have just lost my favorite dog. And to make things worse, it's not just my faith I'm losing. Every morning when I brush my hair, a cascade of blonde strands floats down into the washbasin. Just when the Beattles are popularizing long hair, I'm starting to look like Yul Brynner. This is actual death I'm experiencing, the loss of something that will never return.

Father Nicolas isn't much help. Not with my hair loss, or with my crisis of faith. He keeps telling me that it's only temporary, that I'll get over it.

"This doesn't feel like something I'm going to get over, Father."

The hardest class for me is Father Lyman Fenn's moral theology class. Something about the tone of his voice, its singsong condescension, affects me like a fingernail on a blackboard. For Lyman, the Church is the repository of infallible truth and his job is to feed us that truth in easily digestible, grammar school bites. He knows we aren't buying his outdated message and he masks his rage in a perpetual tight-lipped smile. I sit in a pool of resentment, blocking out his words. I don't want to feel this way about him. I don't trust my negativity and intolerance.

That night I sit at my desk staring at my textbook written in stilted ecclesiastical Latin. My teeth are clenched and there's a knot in my solar plexus. We're only half way through the first semester. How am I going to survive this class? I try to pray about it, firing desperate pleas at my evanescent Jesus. I receive an answer of sorts, an impulse to make one last attempt. I resolve to go into Lyman's class the next day with as open a mind as I can muster. I resolve to listen carefully until I find something, anything, I can agree with and take to heart.

He's lecturing on the cardinal virtues, breaking them down into his usual little pebbles of thought, static little turds that Bergson would characterize as petrifications of *élan vital*. "The cardinal virtues are also called *moral* virtues because they govern our actions, order our passions, and guide our conduct." I see my classmates madly scribbling down phrases: "govern action, order passion, guide conduct." What a waste of time! But then I hear him describing the virtue of Justice: "the determination to give everyone his or her rightful due – honesty, respect."

There it is! That's a truth I can agree with and take to heart. Maybe I've been a hypocrite. I have disliked Lyman Fenn and criticized him, but I've never treated him with honesty and respect. I've certainly never confronted him face to face. I've been acting like a Pharisee.

That evening I walk down to Lyman's room and knock on his door. From deep inside I hear a pleasant "Come in!" Lyman is sitting behind his neatly appointed desk, but he rises and crosses through the haze of cigarette smoke to shake my hand.

"Hello, Greg. How are you?"

I have no stomach for pleasantries tonight. "Well actually, Father, I have something I really need to get off my chest."

"All right. Have a seat." He returns to his desk and calmly draws on his cigarette.

"Father, I know this is my problem, and I'm certainly not trying to tell you how to run your class." I pause, shift in my seat. He smiles and nods. I try to keep smiling myself. "It's just that, after what you said in class today, about how honesty is a person's rightful due, I realize that I need to be straight with you, about my reaction I mean, to some of the things you say."

He smiles at me over his glasses, tents his hands in front of his face.

"Okay" I blurt, "I'm not saying I'm right about this, but we've been exposed to a lot of new ideas in the last few years, and when you throw out your barbs and make fun of these new ideas, well, I find myself pulling down the shades on you. I'm not saying it's good for me to do that. I'm just saying that's what happens to me, and I ... just wanted you to know that."

"Yes," he says, still smiling. "I've noticed that quite a few people are pulling down the shades, especially in your class."

"I'm not trying to tell you how to run your class, Father. I just want to be honest."

Lyman nods. "Well Greg, I certainly thank you for coming forward. This is a very difficult time for the Church and a difficult time for seminarians. But it's also a very dangerous time. I fear we may be on the brink of a schism."

"Gosh, Father, don't you think it's more like the Church will just get more open to different ideas and there'll be a wider spectrum of beliefs?"

"No. I think there's going to be a schism."

We talk a little more and then I rise to leave. He comes around his desk and shakes my hand warmly, thanking me again for having the courage to come and talk to him, man to man. I feel a huge relief. Despite our differences, we have cleared the air, bonded as human beings. I have renewed hope for the seminary and the Church.

# 15

## WHITE SOCK REBELLION

Pope John XXIII dies in June 1963. In less than five years he has changed the Church and our lives forever. He and John F. Kennedy have given us new hope as Catholics. Five months after John XXIII's death, Father Van Antwerp bursts into our Dogmatic Theology class with a radio. "The president's been shot," he says, "where's an outlet?" We spend the rest of the class listening to reports and finally get the awful news, "The President is dead." Afternoon classes are cancelled. I wander out to the field in back of the seminary, aware that everyone in the nation, perhaps the world, is sharing the same thoughts and emotions right now. I begin snapping my fingers, just as I did after my grandmother's death. "Gone, gone, gone," the moments disappearing with each snap. Dead weeds, winter brittle, crunch under my feet. Nothing lasts. It's all just an illusion. When will people realize that?

A letter arrives from the diocese of Santa Rosa. "I am pleased to inform you that the Archbishop has granted your request to transfer to the diocese of Santa Rosa. You will be most welcome to our new diocese." Jim gets the same letter, signed by Bishop Maher. It lifts my mood, but not much. Death is still all around me. My grandfather died last Easter, my dad is failing, my faith is on the rocks. Getting excited about a transfer to another diocese seems childish.

The Beatles are scheduled to appear on the Ed Sullivan show in February, 1964. Early in the week, some of the younger seminarians ask Father Fenn, now the acting rector, if we can watch it. He gives them a fatherly smile. "The Beatles are best watched by hysterical young women, not by mature seminarians." Saturday at supper, Pat Browne slips me a note. "Tobin's lab at 8." Mike Tobin is the resident electronics expert. The faculty has given him a special room in the basement so he can fix their TVs. About fifteen of us sneak down to the basement that night and crowd around a black and white Zenith to watch history being made. Later that year we'll sneak down to another dank basement catacomb to discuss the forbidden books of Jesuit paleontologist Teilhard de Chardin.

Father Wagner dies in April and a couple of days before we leave for summer vacation we hear that our new rector will be Paul Purta, a liberal young priest from a seminary back east. Father Fenn smiles as he makes the announcement, but we know he's not happy with the choice.

That afternoon the faculty makes its appointments for next year's house jobs. Len Duggan runs to the bulletin board as soon as the list goes up. By the time I get there he's grinning at me. "Master of Ceremonies, Mac. You must have some pull."

"Oh God, you're kidding!" That's my idea of Hell – spending two years training other seminarians to bow and genuflect. "Why didn't they pick someone like you who likes that kind of anal stuff?"

My confessor, Father Nicolas, is in charge of the liturgy, so he's the one who arranged this, no doubt hoping to take my mind off my crisis of faith. I see him in the hall after dinner and shake my fist at him. "I'm going to kill you." He smiles and walks off.

That summer I return to the CYO day camp as head counselor. I'm determined to be the best director ever and I encourage the staff to socialize and have fun together. A couple of the older girl counselors are cute and I enjoy teasing them. The exhilaration I feel at camp contrasts sharply with my sober evenings, when I put on my black suit and Roman collar and join Jim and Arnie Kunst taking census in St. Anselm's parish. My dad always smiles when he sees me going out the door in my collar.

We return to the seminary in September, excited about having a progressive rector. Father Purta is of medium height with black curly hair, large dark eyes and a languid mouth. He comes out for Mass the first day dressed in a soft, brightly-colored vestment, hands folded in front of him. When it's time for the homily, he leaves the altar and walks slowly down to the front of the chapel. Opening his lips slightly in the beginning of a smile, he scans first one side of the chapel, then the other. "Good morning and welcome," he says in a resonant voice. He pauses, again sweeping the chapel with his eyes, pew by pew. We all smile back at him, waiting expectantly. "The Church, gentlemen, is going through an exciting but difficult period right now. There are those who feel things are moving too fast, and that we should resist change, hold on to past traditions." He extends his right hand and clenches it into a fist. "On the other hand," and he flails out with his left, "there are those who would rip the Church from its foundations and destroy those traditions in the name of progress." He pauses, then slowly brings his outstretched hands together, cupping them gently in front of his chest. "But if we search between these extremes, we can surely find that delicate balance where tradition will be respected, yet healthy growth fostered at the same time."

"I think he's going to be really good," says Phil Murphy at breakfast. "I remember when he was at St. Joe's, right after he was ordained. He's a good guy."

"He seems open to new ideas," says one of the younger guys, shaking corn flakes into a bowl.

Phil pours coffee into his mug. "He should be. He's only 37. But it'll be interesting to see how he handles the older faculty."

"He seems pretty diplomatic," I say. "He'll probably do all right."

Later I take a walk with Bob Carroll, ask him what he thinks of Purta. "Just another pretty face," Bob says. "We'll see what he actually does."

Actually, Father Purta does quite a bit that first year. He implements the Vatican Council's liturgy decree, he schedules regular meetings with the class presidents, he appoints a student commission to advise him on liturgical matters, he brings in more outside speakers and encourages students to leave the campus for lectures and cultural events. "Priests must become more relevant to modern society," he says, "they need to become more professional."

All this sounds good until one night he announces that, from now on, the nuns will no longer wash white socks, only black ones. "It's too much work for them, separating out the white socks," he says. "We need to make their life easier."

I'm shocked. All my socks are white except for two pairs of black socks that I wear with my suit. Black socks are for squares and they give you athlete's foot. Lots of guys wear white socks. At St. Joe's, we had two nylon mesh bags, one for white socks, one for black. It worked fine. I rendezvous with several of the white sock guys, including Mike Sullivan, a witty jock who is going to be ordained at the end of the year. He and I go up to Purta's room and knock on the door. We hear a "Come in!" and exchange a nervous glance. Purta's at his desk, but stands up and comes around to shake hands with us. He seems friendly and reasonable, so we tell him about our nifty solution to the white sock problem, nylon bags. He nods sympathetically at first but then frowns and looks away. He's no longer listening to us.

"The nuns have too much to do already. You're being inconsiderate."

We give him the health argument, but he doesn't buy it. "You're not thinking of the nuns, you're just thinking of what's convenient for you."

I try to lighten things up a little. "I know! Why don't we outlaw black socks? That way the nuns can just throw the white socks in with our undies.'"

Purta tries to smile, but his upper lip freezes halfway, as if he's about to throw up.

We know the meeting's over, but before we leave Mike lays out our ace in the hole, the card we really hoped we wouldn't have to play. "Okay, Father, you win. We'll just wash them ourselves."

Purta nods slowly, as if he's agreeing, but he still has that nauseated look. Then as he's opening the door for us, he clears his throat. "Look, there's another reason I don't want you wearing white socks."

We wait.

"They don't look professional. They look hunky." Purta smiles and closes the door.

Mike and I exchange looks. "*Hunky?*" he says as we walk back downstairs. "What the Hell does that mean?" "Yeah," I say, "and since when do priests have to look professional? Jesus wasn't a professional. He didn't even wear *shoes*!"

"Well, at least we've found what's bugging him," Mike says. "It has nothing to do with the nuns, the tricky bastard."

We back off, trying to figure out where he's coming from. Norm Dickman is from Chicago, so he's heard of *hunky*. "It's the term people back there use to make fun of Poles. Probably comes from *bohunk* or something."

Okay, that makes sense. Purta's Polish, from back east,

probably the first professional in his family. He's probably sensitive about people making fun of Poles because they worked in the factories and wore white socks.

Several of us wage a silent protest, continuing to wear our hand-washed white socks every day but Sunday. And we keep ribbing Purta about it. In early December he wears a fancy new Advent vestment. "What did you think of it?" he asks a bunch of us after Mass. "It's beautiful," Al Larkin says. "I really like the cut of it."

"I don't know," I say. "To me it looks a little . . . *hunky.*"

At our annual Christmas show, Santa Claus is handing out presents and says, "Oh, what have we here? A present for Father Purta!" He calls Purta up on stage and hands him a package. He unwraps it and finds a pair of white socks. Santa holds up a card. "Oh, and they're the exclusive *Hunky Hose* label." Purta nods and laughs, but I can tell he doesn't like it.

After Christmas vacation he catches me coming out of the dining room one night. "Greg," he says, "during vacation I read a great article about West Point. The cadets there wear socks that are black on top and white on the bottom."

"West Point!" I say. "That's a military academy! They're into discipline for discipline's sake."

He jabs his finger hard into my chest. "Don't forget buddy, once you're ordained you're going to have to follow any orders the bishop gives you."

Suddenly I'm shaking with anger. "Not if they're stupid. If they are, I'll argue with him just like I'm arguing with you."

"We'll see," he says and storms off.

Wow. The gauntlet's been thrown. And it's a sock.

# 16

---

## SEMINARY FILMMAKING

---

It isn't just black socks. Anything that even hints at good ol' boys' clericalism sends me up the wall. Canon Law is the worst. Two thousand picayune, nit-picking regulations are packed into the fat little *Codex Juris Canonici* that serves as our textbook for Dumpy Becker's class. Dumpy is pear-shaped and just as dull as the material he teaches. Out of desperation, we try to liven things up for him. "Father, it says here that priests are always under the jurisdiction of their resident bishop. But what if a priest gets kidnapped by aliens? Does he have to look for a new bishop, or is he still under his old bishop back on earth?" Dumpy gets a slight smile, glad that someone is at least interested enough to ask a question. "Oh, well, I suppose in that case . . ."

He barely finishes when Bob Carroll raises his hand. "Father, we were wondering if we could do a dramatization of the canon about the death of a bishop. We feel it's very important and deserves special attention."

Dumpy looks at his watch. "Oh, well, keep it brief." In no time we've retrieved the wooden coffin we stored in the hall, taped a bishop's mitre on top of it, and are parading around the classroom with candles and holy water, burning incense and chanting the *Dies Irae*. Three years ago I would have disapproved of such childish antics, but now I'm leading the charade. At least I'm still able to laugh. Next semester I will become so disgusted with Canon Law that I'll refuse to study for the final. Dumpy will reluctantly give me a "D," and I'll proudly flaunt it to my classmates.

"I think it's time for us to make another movie," Bob Carroll says. He and I are walking around the grounds with Conrad Gruber and Al Larkin. Al nods his head. "Lots of great shooting locations. The water tower, the archbishop's house."

"Yeah," Conrad says, "have you ever seen all those weird stuffed animals down in the archbishop's basement?"

Nothing happens for a while. We keep talking about particular scenes, but we can't agree on a plot line. Then Bob's dad dies, and there's a big San Francisco funeral, presided over by the archbishop himself. After the ceremony, I get in the receiving line to pay my respects to the family. When I get to Bob, I reach out to shake his hand. "Sorry about your … "

He pulls me into a bear hug and starts whispering in my ear. "Last night in bed, I got it! The plot for our movie. There's a bishop and a crook, see? And they …" He keeps going but I can't concentrate on what he's saying, because we're holding up the whole line and, for God's sake, it's a funeral!

Bob returns to the seminary two days later and hands me a crumpled paper filled with chicken scrawls. It's his outline for the movie: *Greedy bishop counting money. Crook breaks in and tries to steal it. They fight; crook shoots bishop. Cops shoot crook. Bishop's funeral procession. Crook's dead body on wheelbarrow ends up next to bishop's coffin in procession.*

Bob waits for me to finish reading it, then laughs. "We'll call it *A Ballad of the Church and the Modern World.*

Archbishop McGucken's summer house is right next to the seminary. It's a big three-story place with a wrap-around porch in front. Dennis Lucey, who has a key to the place, agrees to leave one of the ground floor windows ajar. That afternoon we go in to have a look. The main floor is polished dark wood, broken only occasionally by floral wallpaper. Colorful portraits of bishops and cardinals in gold leaf frames decorate the walls, juxtaposed with barren lithographs of old European churches. From the spacious front entry we ascend a broad staircase to the second floor. There we find several well-appointed guest rooms and the bishop's own master bedroom. Another staircase leads to a large unfinished attic with loose boards haphazardly scattered across the floor joists. The basement holds a dusty collection of stuffed owls, pelicans, and other wild-eyed birds, along with several dozen more portraits of sallow churchmen who didn't rate an upstairs wall.

A week later, we walk around the Archbishop's house until we're out of sight of the main seminary building, and then double back to the porch and jimmy the window open. Al runs the camera as we film the first scene in the archbishop's bedroom, with Jack Folmer, as a portly bishop, snoring peacefully on McGucken's over-sized Sealy. He's surrounded by prayer books, crucifixes, holy water and a statue of the Virgin Mary. Then we cut to Mike Anderson, a lowlife degenerate, dozing in a seedy room, surrounded by needles, old condoms, and Playboy posters. In the next scene Mike stumbles across the bishop's mansion, breaks in, and finds the bishop in the attic counting a pile of money. After a raucous chase down two flights of stairs, past a gaggle of senile clerics, he kills the bishop in the basement, amidst stuffed birds and gold-framed portraits of anal churchmen.

The filming takes about three weeks and we shoot the funeral procession the last day of the school year, just before the archbishop is due to arrive for his summer vacation.

## MISSISSIPI DEATH WISH

Earlier that year Harvey Cox has published <u>The Secular City</u>, challenging churches to become more relevant to the modern world. It's so popular The Angelus Bookstore in Menlo Park runs out of copies in the first week. Bob Carroll finishes it before I do and waves it at me like Elmer Gantry. "Churches are being bombed in Mississippi and we're sitting around arguing about the length of our surplices. We need to do something real!"

Over the Christmas vacation, at a neighbor's party, I meet Jack, a student from San Francisco State. He's a volunteer for SNCC, and he tells me he's planning to go to Mississippi the next summer to work on voter registration. "Could you use any help?' I ask. "A friend of mine and I might be interested."

Bob and I spend the rest of the school year planning how we can pull off such a stunt, knowing our mothers will have a heart attack if they find out. We decide to tell them we're going on a wilderness camping trip with a couple of our classmates.

"I don't think I've ever heard you mention those boys before," my mother says. "Are they from San Francisco?"

"No, they're both from the Sacramento diocese. They just transferred into St. Pat's last year, so I don't think you've ever met them."

I hate to lie to my mother, but I don't want her to worry. Or to start making phone calls.

The late summer fog has almost burnt off downtown as we board the Greyhound bus marked *Memphis*. Bob shoves his battered duffle bag onto the overhead rack. He looks like he belongs on a bus. His short-sleeve shirt is wrinkled, the pocket stuffed with scribbled notes and a cheap ballpoint pen. His tortoise shell glasses are missing one arm, and a piece of tape covers the nosepiece. Bob is definitely a bus guy.

He plops into the seat beside me and hands me the newspaper he just bought at the station. The headline screams *Race Riot Erupts in Watts* and I feel a twinge in my stomach. "Maybe this isn't the best time to go to Mississippi."

Bob waves off my misgivings. "I'm going to pay most of the expenses on this trip," he says. "My family's a lot wealthier than yours and, as Marx says, 'from each according to his ability to each according to his need.'" I don't argue. It's futile to argue with Bob, especially when he's quoting somebody controversial.

It's dark when the bus finally stops for dinner. Most of the passengers have fallen asleep and the crackle of the driver's microphone jars everyone awake. One guy a few seats ahead leaps up in his seat and slams his head on the luggage rack. "Goddamn! Son of a bitch!" Several drowsy passengers snicker. We stumble off the bus into a deserted station and I head for the restroom.

"This is real," I tell myself as the scent of stale urine hits my nose, "this is the real world. You don't get more relevant than this." I join Bob on a stool in the café and watch the toothless cook peeling hamburgers out of wax paper wrappings, trying to keep up with the sudden influx of orders. The waitress appears with her pencil. "What'll you have, honey?

"Just a piece of apple pie please." My stomach's already cramped up from all that sitting. I don't want a full meal.

I wake up the next morning stiff and sweaty. The early morning light has roused a few other passengers as well, and one woman is trying to pull some food out of a bag on the luggage rack. Bob is still sleeping peacefully. I hear a baby in the back start crying.

"Ever eaten grits before?" We're somewhere in New Mexico and this café is better than the one last night, even though the restroom smells just as bad. Bob mops up the remaining egg yoke with his toast and shakes his head.

"Me neither," I say, "but I like them, especially with this sausage gravy."

Bob pushes his plate aside and pulls out his dog-eared map. "We'll be getting into Memphis pretty late. We may not be able to get a bus down to Shelby until tomorrow morning."

I nod my head. "This bus travel is for the birds."

The guy who hit his head never seems to learn. He sleeps most of the trip and every time the driver announces a stop he pops up like a jack-in-the-box and smacks his head again. "Sonovabitch!" People start waking up early just to watch the show.

Memphis is dark and quiet when the bus pulls in. We walk through a deserted downtown until we see a café with the lights on. A few pickup trucks are parked in the lot out front, most of them with gun racks. A Confederate flag hangs on the wall opposite the front door and the cook is smoking a cigarette down at the end of the counter in front of a black-and-white TV. He looks up at us as we come in, takes another drag on his cigarette, and reaches over for a couple of menus. Several guys in construction caps sit along the counter, sipping their coffee, half-watching the TV. Bob and I slide our bags under a table and sit down. The owner comes over with the menus and a coffee pot and we order some pie. I hear a few guffaws from the counter and look that way. They're laughing at the TV. Amos and Andy. Bob and I look at each other. "Go figure," he says.

The bus to Shelby leaves at nine, just as the heat and humidity are starting to kick in. We head down highway 61 and stop at every little town along the way. Cotton fields stretch out on either side of the highway and here and there we see clusters of Black pickers bent between the rows. Our clothing is damp and sticking to our skin by the time we reach Clarksdale, the birthplace of the blues. It's a nice town, much bigger and more prosperous than the shabby little places we passed along the way. Maybe Shelby will be nice too. I look at the map. Only twenty-five more miles and four more towns. We sail right through Bobo, where there are no buildings, only a crossroads in the middle of a cotton field. Alligator has a few houses and a service station with a little store, so we make a stop there, but no one gets on or off. Duncan is a little bigger, and an elderly Black man in overalls gets slowly off the bus and hobbles over to a waiting car. Five miles south, Hushpuckena doesn't even merit a sign, so I'm relieved when we finally arrive in Shelby and find it's an actual town. We wrestle our duffle bags down from the luggage rack and step down on a hot sidewalk. My back aches and I feel slightly sick. "Feels like we're still moving, doesn't it?" Bob says. Across the street is a prim whitewashed courthouse and several storefronts. People are streaming in and out of the hardware store and several of them cast unfriendly looks our way.

"Let's find Jack, then get something to eat," Bob says, pulling a crumpled piece of paper from his pocket. A pregnant woman pushes a baby carriage down the sidewalk. Bob turns to her, extending the piece of paper. "Excuse me, Ma'am, could you tell us how to get to this address?" The woman hitches up her pedal-pushers and squints at the paper. Then she frowns and jams it back into Bob's hand. "Humph!" She glances down at our duffle bags, and jerks her head abruptly. "That way."

She walks off without saying anything else. "That famous Southern hospitality," I say, and pick up my bag. We head down a tree-lined street with tidy houses set behind white picket fences. Here and there a Confederate flag waves from a front porch pillar. We walk for several blocks past neat houses and manicured lawns. There is no sign of activity, everything locked into quiet stillness by the oppressive heat. The sidewalk ends suddenly and the road turns to dirt. The houses are still neat and well maintained, but sewage now flows in open gutters next to the road. There are no more street lights. "Looks like we're getting closer," Bob says. "If you're Negro, you don't get any city services for your property taxes."

A lot more people are outside in this part of town. An elderly Black woman is sweeping her porch and waves to us. Bob waves back. "Hi. Could you tell us how to find Strand Road?"

"Why sure, honey. You almost there. Next block down you'll see the sign." She wipes her arm across her forehead. "Are you here to help with the voter registration?"

"Yes Ma'am, we sure are." Bob's already drawling like a Southerner.

"Well God bless you."

Strand Road is at the edge of town, much more rural than the streets we've been walking. Its few houses are more like shacks and behind them stretch acres and acres of cotton. There's a pickup in front of one of the shacks and some children are sitting on the rickety porch. Their eyes get big as we walk up. "Hi," I say. "Does a man named Jack live around here?"

The smaller kids just stare at me, but an older boy says, "He over there," pointing to a door at the other end of the porch. We knock and hear a muffled "Come in" from inside. Jack is stretched out on a sleeping bag in the corner of the room. Next to him is a wooden box on its side with some underwear stacked inside and a few books and papers on top.

"Hey, you made it," he says, rubbing his eyes. "I was just catching a nap. I didn't get back until late last night. We had a SNCC meeting down in Greenville." He pulls his lanky body up from the floor, tucks his blue workshirt into frayed jeans. "Put your stuff over there. This is where we sleep, that other room back there is sort of a kitchen. The john's on the back porch. Did you meet the kids? They live in the other half of the house with their mom and sometimes her boyfriend."

I put my bags down and walk into the other room. There's a faucet and sink at one end and a table with a hotplate next to it. In the near corner is a homemade set of shelves with a few pots and dishes. A door leads out to the back porch, a narrow ledge about three feet wide with an outhouse on one end. The shithole sits directly over a little stream running along the back of the house out to the fields.

I come back into the main room. "No refrigerator?"

"No," Jack says. "Most of the poor Negroes can't afford them. Which is convenient for the good ole boys in the welfare office. When they hand out the commodity foods from the government, they hold back the butter and bacon and eggs because they say the Negroes lack proper refrigeration. They keep all that good stuff for themselves and give the Negroes the powdered milk and cornmeal."

"You're kidding! How can they get away with that?" I ask.

Jack laughs. "You won't believe what goes on down here. Growing up in the Bay Area, no one has any idea. I sure didn't. These people have no rights at all. They can be thrown in jail for anything, and they have no due process rights. Same with us. You never want to go out in the truck by yourself, because the cops can charge you with anything, and if you don't have a witness, you're screwed."

"Sounds like you're screwed even if you do have a witness."

"Well, there are a lot of federal lawyers down here now, watching for civil rights violations, so things are better than they were. But you still have to watch out for the Klan. They love to arrange accidents for freedom riders."

Someone's banging on the door. "The kids," says Jack. "They want to know what's going on. Let's go next door and meet Effie."

The kids crowd around us on the porch. "Is your mama awake?" asks Jack.

"Mama! Jack here to see you," yells a chorus of voices. One of them opens the door and we enter a room identical to the one on our side of the house. A large Black woman is lying on an old metal bed. The mattress sags under her weight and several pillows are propped under her head. She's watching a soap opera on an old black and white TV. Several old quilts are strewn around the floor and a couple more kids lie on one of them.

"Wanted you to meet some friends of mine, Effie. Bob

and Greg will be working with me for a while, staying next door."

Effie stays on the bed and lifts a heavy arm. "All right then, nice to meet you boys. I'd get up, but I been pickin' all week and I can hardly stand."

"That's all right, Effie," says Jack. "You just get yourself some rest. Come on kids, time to play outside."

We walk a few blocks to a low batten-board house with a small garden in front. The door is open and a small woman wearing a kerchief comes out. She has a bowl in one hand and a knife in the other. "Supper will be ready in about half an hour," she says. "You come back then."

"They take turns cooking for us," Jack explains. "Minnie does it a couple of times a week. She's got a son who works for SNCC down in Jackson."

The next morning a mosquito wakes me up, I can hear it in my ear, trying to bore through the t-shirt I pulled over my head last night. I pull the t-shirt off and taste the hot, muggy air carrying rank odors from the outhouse. On the floor next to me, Bob's sleeping with a slung open mouth and a hand across his forehead like he's warding something off. I close my eyes, my lids still hot from sleep. Through the wall I can hear Ricky Ricardo yelling "Lucy!!" in his high-pitched voice. It's surreal. Why am I here? Yes, I'm doing something noble for my fellow man, but there's something else going on, something that's been gnawing at the edges of my brain through nine states and forty hours of hot grueling Greyhound. What I haven't told Bob, what I can't tell my hope-blind mother or my stroke-bound father, what I can barely admit to myself, is that I have traveled 2000 miles to the boondocks of Mississippi in my 24th year because I want to escape. I want to outrun a looming decision. I open my eyes. A buzzing fly is frantically bouncing off the window pane. Outside a kid is crying, another is laughing. The truth is I'm using this place, hoping something will happen down here to disrupt my future. Maybe I'll get shot or beaten and a hero's waiver will set me free. The fact is, I've come all this way because I'm not sure I really want to be ordained as a priest.

# 18

## CHRISTIAN PREJUDICE

The next day we load a bunch of Black teenagers into the old Ford pickup and drive them down to Greenfield for a non-violent defense workshop. Young Black activists teach them about Ghandi, show them how to curl up in a ball and wrap their arms around their heads when the police start clubbing them. Next morning we pick up six elderly Black women, put blankets down in the truck bed for them, and drive them down to Jackson where they will register to vote for the first time. I listen to Jack giving them last minute instructions. "Remember, they can't require you to take a literacy test. They'll tell you they can, but the new Civil Rights Act has changed that. If they don't let you register, for whatever reason, you come right out and tell one of our lawyers." They nod, but shoot nervous glances at each other.

I've never felt hate before, but here it's palpable. Bob and I walk downtown to the grocery the next morning and every white person we pass stares at us with dull, lazy-eyed revulsion. Even the kids. We come up on two little boys laughing and wrestling with each other. They see us and their mouths curl down. They must practice that look.

It's so ugly. I don't want to be here. I want to be back home, back on Strand Road with my little Black friends.

"Let's try going to Mass," Bob suggests. "There's got to be at least one liberal Catholic in this town." The church is new, but the statues are old, traditional. A large crucifix dominates the altar, blood oozing from the thorns on Christ's head. We sit near the back, saying the prayers with the congregation, standing and kneeling with them, processing up for Communion. No one seems to notice us. Maybe none of these people know who we are. After Mass we genuflect and head toward the door. A plump, red-faced woman in a lime polyester pantsuit rushes up and blocks our way. She waves her missal in Bob's face. "You should be ashamed of yourselves!" Her voice is quaking with rage. Other parishioners hear her and head toward us. "Coming down here to stir up trouble. What kind of Catholics are you anyway?" The pastor is standing just outside the door, greeting parishioners. He looks over and nods his agreement. "Actually we're seminarians," I say, "and I think if Jesus were alive today, He'd be demonstrating for civil rights."

"Communists is what you are," the woman wails. We push past her toward the pastor. He won't meet our eyes.

Later we're at a strategy meeting at Fred Brown's house. He's the local registration coordinator and he breaks into a huge grin when we tell him what happened. "Brother, if you waitin' for the churches to step forward, you gonna have a long wait." The other Blacks around the kitchen table nod their agreement. "Those good ol' white boys, they've got all the ministers, even the Negro ones, on their payroll, 'long with all the school principals. Ain't none of those folks going to tell people to vote. They got too much to lose."

Bob and I go to the local Black church next Sunday to see for ourselves. About thirty people, mostly elderly, are standing in the blazing sun in front of a drab clapboard church. They are dressed in freshly washed, if slightly frayed, Sunday clothes, fanning themselves with worn paper fans. The pastor rolls up forty-five minutes late in a long shiny Cadillac, wearing a fancy baby-blue suit. He pries himself out of the passenger seat, surveys his congregation, and heads toward the church. "Excuse me, Pastor," says Bob, intercepting him, "we were wondering if sometime during the service we could announce next week's voter registration drive." The pastor barrels straight ahead, dismissing him with a pudgy hand. "No politics in the house of the Lord."

Inside, he dons a bright blue robe, eases himself into a cushioned chair. He nods brusquely toward the rear of the church and the choir bursts into song and begins to move jauntily up the aisle. Most of them are young, and the women sway their hips and breasts in time to the music, their glistening chocolate skin highlighted by the azure blue robes. They make their way slowly through the congregation and up to the sanctuary to their places in the choir stall. The pastor looks them up and down as they pass, running his tongue around moist smiling lips, like a wolf eyeing sheep. His eyes are half-mast and dreamy, as if he's imagining taking one to bed.

After each hymn the pastor gets up and preaches, coaxing more money for the collection basket each time. "Seven collections," Bob whispers. "That's worse than the Catholics!" The pastor sits down again. "If any feel the Spirit moving you, stand now and testify." He closes his eyes, nodding his approval as several people stand up and praise the Lord for favors received. When there's a pause, I see Bob getting to his feet, hands extended toward Heaven. "We thank thee, Heavenly Father for all your gifts," he says in a booming voice. The pastor's eyes open a slit and I see beady pupils darting around under big turtle lids. "And we especially thank you, Father, for giving us the chance to register to vote this coming week. We thank you and bless your name. Amen." Bob sits down and the pastor, glaring, gestures the choir to start singing.

# 19

## KLAN CAPERS

Later that week I drive a group of teenage boys to a workshop. The old truck's steering is loose, veering first to one side then to the other, so I'm concentrating on the road. I don't notice the bright yellow Impala coming up behind me until it pulls in next to me and honks. Two men are leaning out the windows waving their middle fingers at me. "Hey Nigger lover, pull over." I push down the accelerator and get ahead of them, straddling the white line so they can't get around. In the rear-view mirror I count five of them, all in their 30s or 40s. The kids are yelling now, flipping them off. We haven't learned any non-violent strategies for this kind of situation. I start praying, yelling really, "Lord, help us, dammit! Show me what to do!" I look into the mirror just in time to see one of my kids holding up an empty coke bottle. He waves it at the Impala, then launches it in a graceful arc. I see smoke erupt from under the Impala's tires as it dips forward into a violent skid. The bottle shatters on the asphalt just in front of it.

Oh shit, we're really screwed now! I jam the accelerator to the floor and glance again at the mirror, expecting to see the Impala roaring up on us. Instead, it grows smaller in the distance. Then it turns around and heads off in the other direction. I gulp air. "Whew! Thanks, Lord, for the clarification: communication trumps principle." Non-violence didn't impress those guys, but that coke bottle sure did.

We get the warning a few days later. The local Black leaders tell us the Klan is planning to bomb our house, probably over the weekend. They arrange for Effie and her kids to sleep somewhere else and recommend we do the same. Friday evening we grab our toothbrushes and walk through the dusty streets to a little dance joint Jack knows about. Kids run past us, playing tag in the twilight. Smells of salt pork and beans waft from open doors. We hear music and see a small clapboard building with a handwritten sign over the door, *Fanny's Place*. We open the screen door and walk onto a lively dance floor. The music's coming from an old jukebox on one wall. On the other end of the room is a bar with a grill and a beer cooler. We stash our duffle bags in one corner and make our way to the bar. Lithe bodies move to the beat of Muddy Waters. Fanny hands us beers from the cooler and throws three patties on the grill. I watch the girls on the dance floor throwing their hips in tight-fitting cotton dresses, arms and shoulders glistening with sweat. What would it feel like to move like that? I think of the beer-bellied Klansmen in their Impala, the woman at Mass waving her missal, my seminary professors. None of them could move like that. None of them know this kind of freedom and joy. I catch a glimmer of another world, pulsing with life and sexual energy. I want that. I'm here in Mississippi as a savior, a crusader, a warrior. I want to be a dancer, a lover.

At sunrise, the dancing finally winds down and we head back to our house. The glow of the rising sun confers a majesty on the dusty cotton fields to the east, and we walk through the long shadows cast by pickers' low-slung shanties. As we turn into Strand Road, I scan the houses, counting down to where ours should be.

Yes! It's still there. "I guess we're safe until tonight," says Jack. "Let's get some sleep." The floor feels good under my weary bones and I fall asleep immediately. I awake around 10 a.m., after dreaming about the Impala and the coke bottle. Something stirs in my consciousness, a plan. I get up quickly, careful not to wake the others, and head downtown. The hardware store is bustling, lots of pickups parked out front. The old screen door squeaks when I push it open. There are customers by the counter with soda bottles in their hands, a few are over at the tool rack. Everyone turns when the door slams shut behind me. The store goes completely silent. All their eyes are on me. Behind the counter the man at the cash register straightens and clears his throat. "Can I help you?" His tone is mocking. My heart is beating wildly. I cross the floor in slow deliberate steps. I look at the cashier. He's tall and bald and his Adam's apple goes up and down in a slow swallow. I say loudly, "I'd like a box of .22 shells please." His eyes open wide, then he catches himself, turns around and slowly reaches for a box of shells. "That'll be two dollars and fifty nine cents."

I lay three bills on the counter. "Thank you." I can feel all eyes on me. I collect my change and walk back to the door, doing my best gunfighter swagger, a skinny John Wayne with thinning hair and glasses.

Bob is just waking up when I get back. I toss the shells down on the wooden box next to the bed and tell him what I just did. He sits up in bed. His orange curls are smashed down on one side and his eyes look naked without his thick glasses. He rubs the bridge of his nose.

"That was really stupid," he says. "You've violated every principle of the civil rights movement. Now the Klan's really going to be pissed."

I'm used to Bob getting mad, especially when someone hasn't followed his script. "We didn't violate any principles," I say. "We don't even have a gun. I just want to bluff these boneheads and see what happens."

The Klan backs off, but Sunday afternoon another problem arises. Jack bursts into the house and says, "Come on! We need to take a ride." He guns the truck onto the main road. "Fred Brown's out of town at a meeting, so we need to take care of this. Mrs. Johnson got arrested this morning right after church and they've got her in jail charged with robbery."

"Who's Mrs. Johnson?" asks Bob.

"She's just a very nice, very straight-laced Negro lady in her fifties who works as a housekeeper for a senile old white woman in town. She's raised a family, goes to church every Sunday and has never been in trouble in her life."

"What's she doing in jail then?"

"That's the thing. The old lady lost a ten dollar bill and told the police that her housekeeper must have stolen it, so they came and arrested her on her way out of church this morning. There's no way Mrs. Johnson would ever steal anything."

"What are we going to do?" I ask.

"Go make sure she's okay. Then we'll write up the case for SNCC." He turns left and heads west.

"I thought the jail was downtown," Bob says.

"That's the White jail. The one with windows and lights and heat. She's in the Colored jail out by the river."

We pull up to an old brick structure that looks deserted. Metal bars crisscross the open windows and door. A figure clutches the bars at the door. As we approach I see that she is dressed in a nice dress and is wearing a hat with flowers on it.

"Hi Mrs. Johnson. I'm Jack Scofield and this is Bob and Greg. How are you?"

"I'm scared to death," she says glancing toward the back of the jail. "I saw a rat run across the floor over there and I heard noise coming from one of those straw mattresses. I've heard there's snakes in here from the river."

"Are you here all alone?" I ask.

"Yes sir."

"Did they give you any food?"

"Are you kidding? Jack snorts. "They don't give Negro prisoners anything. We'll bring you some food, Mrs. Johnson."

"How long will I be here? Will I have to stay overnight?" She's shaking, trying to hold back tears.

"I don't know," says Jack. "But we'll do everything we can."

We return later with a hamburger from Fanny's and a coke. She's still standing at the door.

"Thank you boys, but I don't think I could eat anything right now. I'm too upset."

Our calls to the sheriff prove fruitless. "He won't be in until tomorrow morning," the answering service says. "You'll just have to call back then."

When we return to the jail the next morning, Mrs. Johnson is still standing where we left her, still clutching the bars, her eyes red and puffy, but her dress and hat still in place.

A few days later Jack gets pulled over and thrown in jail in Greenville. The sheriff there is infamous for using a cattle prod on prisoners, so Bob and I hitch a ride down there as soon as we can. The sheriff smirks at us as he adds his bogus jail expenses to the bail fee. "You boys come down here stirring up all this trouble, you gotta expect a little trouble in return."

Jack walks out looking very relieved. "Last night they threw me in with a couple of rednecks and said, 'Here's another one of them freedom riders.' Those same guys beat up a civil rights worker in that cell a couple nights ago, and they were threatening to cut me up with a broken mirror. I kept telling them my lawyer was on the way, so luckily they didn't try anything."

---

## DISILLUSIONMENT

---

Bob and I return from Mississippi near the end of August, just a week before we're due back at the seminary. There is a message waiting for me that Father Durkin has invited a couple of us to visit him at his new parish in downtown San Francisco. Durkin was the assistant pastor at my parish for a couple of years and is a friend of Pat Browne. He's a big cynical guy who always delights in shattering the idealistic illusions of his seminary proteges by exposing us to the "realities" of the priesthood. He regularly tells us scandalous stories about other priests, brags about how he made $300 in Mass stipends on Mothers' Day alone. He prides himself as a traditionalist who lives by the book, and he has no use for his fellow priests who work with the poor or dedicate themselves to migrant worker ministries or other causes. "They're fanatics," he says.

We arrive at the rectory in the heart of downtown and walk up to a locked gate with a sign instructing us to go to an adjacent telephone booth and call a certain number. We go to the booth and find it's a pay phone, that we need a dime. A gruff voice answers, "Yea, what do you want?"

"We're seminarians, here to see Father Durkin."

The voice softens a little. "Okay, go over by the gate and I'll let you in." A guy in a police uniform comes out with a ring of keys and unlocks the heavy gate. He points through the vestibule. "The elevator is on your left. Father Durkin is on three."

As we ascend, Pat tells us about the parish. "There are five stories in this place, six if you count the shooting gallery in the basement. Four priests live here, each one on his own floor. The kitchen and dining room are on the first floor, and the pastor has the top story."

"Sounds like a jolly place," I say. "What's this about a shooting gallery?"

"The pastor's a bit nuts," Pat says. "He's got a BB gun that he uses to shoot bums who come up on the church steps. He practices his aim in the basement."

Durkin meets us at the elevator. "Gentlemen! Welcome to the inner city." He walks us into his room, a dismal affair with very few books and a lot of photos of him in his collar. "It's great to be back in the city," he says.

"Why?" asks one of the others. "You're right in middle of the slums."

"Actually, St. Joseph's is one of the best-endowed parishes in the city," Durkin says. "Even the people who moved away still come back for church. And the Mass stipends are triple what they are in suburbia. Plus I get to wear this." He pulls back his coat sleeve to reveal a small billy club strapped to his wrist. "We have a lot of security here. That guy at the front door is an off-duty cop. Lots of locks." He pulls out a key ring with about thirty keys on it.

I'm starting to get a headache. "Do you have a soup kitchen or anything for all the poor people around here?"

"The bums? No they go to St. Vincent's. McCarthy shoots them if they hang around here. That's his favorite night-time activity."

I shake my head. This is unbelievable, priests armed against their parishioners, a pastor *shooting*, rather than *feeding*, his flock? What kind of twisted, psychotic religion is this? Have these guys never read the Gospels? Do they even remember who Jesus was?

We visit a little longer, then take the elevator back down to the cop's desk and he lets us out. In the car, the other guys are joking about the rectory, laughing about the pastor's shooting gallery. I can't laugh. The place symbolizes everything that's wrong with Catholicism, and they don't see it. I realize I no longer share their goals, their values, or their assumptions about God and the Church. I've become an outsider, a heretical quisling within the system. It's a lonely role, though at the same time, strangely exhilarating. I am once again my grandmother's protege, fighting a world full of apathy and sloth. I can feel her warrior energy in my veins, though I suspect she would neither recognize, nor approve of, my current battle flag.

# 21

---

## RE-ENTRY

---

In August 1965, President Lyndon Johnson makes it illegal to burn your draft card. A month later the Vatican Council issues its decree on religious freedom, Willie Mays hits his 500th home run, and the Haight Ashbury declares a form of religious freedom that the Vatican never had in mind. Bob and I are back from Mississippi radicalized and ready for bear.

Mrs. Pulskamp drives Jim and me down to the seminary on a balmy September afternoon. Always before, the return seemed familiar, reassuring, but today it has a surreal quality about it. We turn off Middlefield Road and drive up the wooded lane. The red brick seminary looms ominously. The statue of St. Patrick on the front lawn seems to reproach me for some unspoken crime. Jim and his mother feel like strangers. I see classmates unloading cars, laughing and joking. God, they're blind to the real world, shuttered into this pitiful little world of rules and rubrics. Leonard Duggan walks up to me, already wearing his cassock even though it's not required until dinner. "Hey, Mac, did you hear? Sheehan quit." Leonard has that smug *I-told-you-so* look on his face that makes me want to slug him. We used to be good friends at St. Joe's, but now he's become one of Father Fenn's right-wing proteges.

I'm not surprised to hear about Sheehan. Tom's prodigious intellect and liberal ideas have often gotten him in trouble with the faculty and they "clipped" him last year, refusing him the next level of religious orders. "So who do you think will take his place as class president?" Leonard asks, savoring my displeasure.

"Maybe you should run, Leonard. You could take us back to the Council of Trent."

He laughs. "Sure, Mac."

A week later I'm elected class president.

## CONTROVERSY

On our way back from our voter registration efforts in Mississippi, Bob Carroll and I had talked a lot about the lack of *due process,* not only in the South, but also in the seminary. Now, the more I think about it, the more outraged I get. As seminarians, we have no individual rights. We can be thrown out at any time, with no explanation, unable to defend ourselves against unknown accusers. It happened to Pete Martinez a few years back. Someone found a note to a girl in what he thought was Pete's handwriting, and without telling Pete, reported him to the prefect of discipline. The next day Pete was called into the rector's office, given a bus ticket and told to leave the seminary. The fact that it wasn't his note didn't make any difference.

As part of his liberal agenda, Father Purta schedules a monthly dialogue with the class presidents. I disrupt every meeting with a harangue about our due process rights. "Greg," Father Purta calmly responds, "you have to remember that the Catholic Church is not a democracy." That really sets me off.

In October Bob and I schedule an underground screening of *A Ballad of the Church and the Modern World* in the seminary basement. About thirty guys show up, including most of those who acted in it. They all laugh and seem to enjoy themselves, but a week later the shit hits the fan. Ken Kelzer has a dour expression as he walks up and hands me a piece of paper. "We've formed a committee," he says. "Many of us in the movie were not aware of the whole context and we feel our rights have been violated." I look at the list of names. Most had bit parts, but there are a couple of others who weren't in the film at all, whom I don't even remember attending the screening. "We're demanding a meeting. We want the movie destroyed."

"You what?" I start to laugh. "You want it destroyed?" He's not smiling. I hand him back the paper. "We'll meet with you, but there's no way we're going to destroy the movie."

"Tomorrow night at seven in the theology classroom," he says and walks off.

Bob is thrilled when I tell him. "Our own inquisition," he says. "I wonder if they'll want to burn us."

I'm perplexed by their reaction. It's true we didn't spell out the whole plot, but most of them were in the archbishop's house during the filming and saw Jack Folmer dressed as a bishop being chased down the stairs by Mike Anderson with a gun. What did they think it was, a catechism video? And what about the other two guys on the committee, the ones who didn't even see the film? Why have they been so quick to jump on an issue they aren't even involved in?

The pieces of the puzzle fall into place a few days later

when Leonard Duggan walks up with his usual smug grin. "Hey, Mac, I was talking to my pastor yesterday and he said Jim Halligan told him some seminarians made a dirty movie about the archbishop." His smile gets wider. "A lot of the clergy are pretty worked up about it."

Jim Halligan was Mike Anderson's cousin, and now I remember that he accompanied Mike to the first preview of the movie during the summer. Though he passed himself off as a liberal and said he really enjoyed the movie, he evidently started calling his friends as soon as he got home. By now the clergy gossip mill is running full speed, which explains the presence of those two plants on the committee.

The four of us enter the theology classroom and see the eight committee members already sitting in a tense semi-circle. We pull in chairs to complete the circle and Ken clears his throat. "Thanks for coming. We're here to express our grievances and to suggest a solution." They go around the circle, saying how upset they are, how they feel betrayed and lied to. They all agree that the only solution is to destroy the movie.

We sit silently until they're finished. Then Bob says, "Thanks for sharing." A couple of them smile, getting his attempt at humor. The rest sit stone-faced. "But we never lied to you," he says. "We just didn't tell you the whole plot."

"Although," I jump in, "most of you certainly saw enough to be able to figure it out."

Jerry Kennedy cuts me off, pulling rank as the deacon

class president. "This thing is an embarrassment to the whole seminary. Something has to be done about it, and fast."

"Did you see the movie, Jerry?" I ask.

"No, but I've heard enough about it to know it's totally inappropriate."

"Well," says Bob, ignoring Jerry and addressing the rest of them. "I'm glad that you've spoken up about this. We understand your feelings and here's what we're willing to do. Every time we show the film we'll announce that many of the actors were duped into participating and that they wish to disassociate themselves from its content. We'll even put it in writing. As far as your demand that we destroy the movie, well that's censorship, and last time I looked this is the twentieth century. That's where we stand." We walk out, leaving the committee huddled in righteous outrage. I suggest to Bob that we hide the real film and put a dummy on my desk, in case they try to steal it.

Two days later, Ken hands me a letter, signed by the members of the committee. *"We are disappointed by your refusal to take appropriate action on this issue. We had hoped to solve the problem as brothers in Christ. However, failing that, we feel we must bring this issue to a higher authority. We have scheduled an appointment with Father Purta for next Satuday morning at nine o'clock. At that time, we will present the whole case, including names and content. You are free to attend that meeting if you wish." "In Christ,"* is followed by their signatures.

"Great!" I tell the others. "I'm going to that meeting! I want to see Purta's face when they tell him. See if he believes in free speech or not."

I'm actually looking for a way out, hoping someone else will make the priesthood decision for me. It's not that I don't want to be a priest. I just don't believe in organized religion any more. Bob says he won't attend. Unbeknown to me, he's already decided to leave the seminary at the end of the semester, so he's not interested in playing any more hierarchy games. Al and Conrad are unwilling to go as well, though it's more complex for them. They support the position we've taken, but they also want to be priests. If Father Purta is officially informed, he may feel obliged to expel all of us. That would be devastating for Al and Conrad. Best for them to lay low.

Tension builds as Saturday approaches. Jim Kidder explodes at me in the hall on Thursday. "Gregory, don't be stupid! There was a condom in that movie. That means you had to buy the condom, which is a mortal sin. Condoms are inherently evil. They have only one purpose – sin. Why are you being so stubborn?"

"I beg to differ," I say. "Condoms have at least one other purpose. As props in a movie."

"Keep thinking that way," he says, "and you'll end up in Hell."

It's Friday night when Jack Folmer knocks on my door. His face is flushed and there are dark circles under his eyes. "I'm sorry Greg, but I can't stand this," he says. "If you guys don't do something, I'm going to have to leave the seminary." Tears well up in his eyes and he looks away. I touch his shoulder. "Okay, Jack. It's okay. I'll talk to Bob."

By the time I get to Bob's room, I have an idea for a solution. He agrees and we tell Ken to call his committee together. Only five of them show up. Bob sits off to the side, his face bright red. He's too angry to talk. I scan their faces, see fear there. "Let's get one thing clear," I say. "What we're about to propose is for Jack, not in response to what we consider your groundless fears and concerns. Because of Jack's discomfort, we're willing to declare a five-year moratorium. We won't show the movie for five years, by which time all of you will either be ordained or will have left the seminary. That's what we're willing to do. For Jack, not for you. If you don't like it, go report us to Purta."

To my personal disappointment, they call off the meeting with Purta.

## POLITICS & GUERILLA THEATER

Ever since Mississippi, Bob and I have been waging a two-man civil rights campaign in the seminary. After watching Father Purta adroitly divide and conquer the six class presidents, we demand that the entire student body be represented by a single elected president, knowing it's the only way our liberal agenda will stand a chance.

Just before Christmas, Bob knocks on my door. "I've decided to leave," he says. "I won't be coming back after vacation." He's the last political ally I have in my class. "Man, can't you wait 'til the end of the year? What am I going to do without you?" He smiles and shrugs. "Sorry."

The rest of my classmates are so excited about being ordained deacons in June that they could care less about their civil rights. Pat Browne and I walk around one evening and he shakes his head. "McAllister, if you keep up this radical shit, you're going to get your ass thrown out of here." I look over at him. He's a company man. He doesn't understand that I don't care if I get thrown out. In fact, I'd welcome it.

The younger classmen tend to be more radical. Instead of reading Pius Parsch and "Theology Today," they've been listening to the Beatles and Bob Dylan: *The times, they are a changin'*. I spend many Thursday holidays drinking beer with them at the Round Table Pizza Parlor in Palo Alto, plotting the seminary revolution. I become their candidate for student body president. It's a long-shot. Three of the four other candidates are moderates, echoing Purta's call for balance. One is more reactionary than the Vatican. During the candidates' debate, I find myself way out in left field and it seems highly unlikely I can woo the simple majority necessary to win.

Sunday, March 13th is voting day. Leonard Duggan grins and holds up his ballot just before he puts it in the box. He's written *Non Placet!!* in large letters. He's protesting the whole idea of a student body president, probably reflecting the views of his confessor, Father Fenn. How many more feel that way?

Late that evening the final count is posted on the bulletin board. As I walk up, Phil DeAndrade claps me on the back. 'Congratulations! It's a landslide." Of 133 votes cast, I have 79, sixty more than my closest rival. As unlikely as it seems, I have received a mandate.

Father Purta waits for me to come out of the refectory the next day and gives me one of his dead fish handshakes. "Congratulations, Greg. I look forward to working with you." He's wearing his nausea smile again. Caught between a conservative archbishop and an unpredictable bunch of seminarians, the last guy he wanted as student body president was Greg McAllister.

"The archbishop's coming down to celebrate his silver

anniversary next week," he says. "I want you to present him with a gift on behalf of the student body. And do you suppose you could arrange some entertainment for him too, maybe one of your skits?" In the last couple of years, I've moved from pranks to satirical skits in an attempt to leaven our tense seminary politics with some Bergson humor.

That afternoon, Gil Mata pulls me aside. "You know what Purta's up to, don't you? He's hoping you'll put on some radical skit and he'll be able to say to the archbishop, 'See what I'm dealing with here?' Believe me, it's a setup."

I go to the chapel, sit in the silence and think long and hard about the skit. I even talk to Jesus about it, even though I'm not sure He's really there. Then it comes to me. We'll do a skit where we make fun of everybody, and we'll start with ourselves. It'll be a catharsis for all the pent-up anger and anxiety everyone's been feeling. I run up to Gil's room and knock on the door. I hear the bed squeak and he opens the door rubbing his eyes.

"Sorry, I was resting my eyes," he says grinning.

"I'm glad you warned me about Purta and the skit," I say. "But we're still going to do it." He looks at me skeptically. "And you're going to be in it."

Gil has worked with Father Purta a lot, even written some of his speeches for him, so he knows how he thinks and talks. He's the natural choice to play the rector in *Everyseminarian, A Morality Play.*

The refectory has been transformed for the archbishop's anniversary dinner. Brightly colored banners hang from the walls, fresh wildflowers grace each student table, and a huge bouquet of roses highlights a delicately embroidered tablecloth on the faculty table. Archbishop McGucken sits at the center, flanked by Father Purta and Father Fenn. One hundred and sixty seminarians shovel down steak and potatoes and steal excited glances at the elevated platform where their elders preside. After dessert, Father Purta rings the bell and stands up. "We want to welcome you, Archbishop, and congratulate you on this, your silver anniversary as a priest. We feel extremely fortunate to have such a wise and inspiring leader in our midst." The archbishop smiles and nods to our applause. "And now I will turn the program over to our newly-elected student body president, Greg McAllister." The archbishop turns my way, smiling politely. I return his smile. "Good evening, Archbishop. In honor of your anniversary, we have prepared some entertainment for you. In the best medieval tradition, we present a brief morality play entitled *Everyseminarian.*"

I point the other side of the refectory where John Van Hagen, as Everyseminarian, ascends a small stage. There he is set upon by the vice of Rashness, urging him to take a radical stand with the rector. In the nick of time, the virtue of Prudence intervenes, dispelling Rashness and counseling restraint. Rashness returns, however, and prevails. The scene ends with Everyseminarian yelling, "I demand to see Father Purta!"

Scene Two: The Rector's office. Everyseminarian crashes in, yelling, "The students demand the right to have dogs in our rooms!" Gil Mata, playing Purta, sits upright on a chair. Behind him stands Big Bob Johnson swathed in a sheet and holding a broomstick with pie-plate scale pans suspended from each end. The Rector says, "Well, John, on the one hand I appreciate your concern … " and starts leaning to the left. Dame Balance gives him a nudge back toward center. "On the other hand, you have to be aware … " tilting now to the right. Balance keeps nudging him back and forth as he presents first one, then the other, side of the issue. Finally he lands in the middle. "But I think we can achieve a delicate balance between these two positions."

I look over at the faculty table. Purta is turning red; the archbishop is smiling broadly.

Scene Three: The Archbishop's office. This is the scene we've all been waiting for. Dennis Lucey has a perfect imitation of the Archbishop, so perfect that even Father Purta often genuflects and pretends to kiss Dennis' ring when he passes him in the hall, just so Dennis will do his archbishop imitation. Now Dennis ascends the stage dressed in bishop's robes. There is laughter from the floor, then silence as seminarians steal nervous glances toward the Archbishop, wondering if this is going to work. Dennis sits in a chair, a telephone next to him. There's a knock at the door and the Rector enters. "Your Excellency, I'm sorry to trouble you with such trivial matters, but I have a request from the seminarians." The Archbishop beckons him in, but just then, the phone rings. "Excuse me, Father," Dennis says in McGucken's unmistakable brogue. He picks up the phone. "Oh yes, Hello Leo, how are things up in the Redwood Empire?" It's Bishop Maher on the line. "Oh, I'm sorry to hear that, Leo ... yes ... yes. Well, you know the old saying: *Roma locuta est, causa finita est.*" There's a slight pause, then Dennis frowns and says, "What do you mean, 'what does that mean?'"

Archbishop McGucken lets out a loud guffaw and the whole place breaks into relieved hysterics. We all know Leo flunked first high Latin. Dennis has chosen the perfect foil for his spoof.

I look around the room and feel the cathartic energy. The archbishop, Father Purta, the faculty, the students, we're all laughing together. Hard. We've broken through the distrust and fear. We've found our common humanity through laughter.

Thank you, Lord. This is the priesthood I want.

## DOUBLE STANDARDS

The living room of the Bishop's new mansion is spacious, easily accommodating the thirty or so priests who have gathered here after their annual retreat. Two bars, one at either end of the room, are churning out cocktails, mainly scotch or bourbon, to the boisterous crowd. Jim Pulskamp and I are the only seminarians here, invited to dinner by the bishop, since we'll soon be joining this fraternity as fellow priests. I stand by the large picture window and gaze down at a rolling lawn and a kidney-shaped swimming pool. Directly across from me, a grotto of the Blessed Virgin catches the afternoon sun. I turn as Bishop Maher's nasal voice cuts through the chatter.

"Welcome to the first of many events in this beautiful place." Leo raises his glass. "And don't be shy at the bar. This is our compensation for celibacy. Drink up!" Everyone laughs and raises their glasses.

Next to me, Pat Flynn mutters in his County Mayo brogue to a group of fellow pastors. "*Emperor Leo's* a good name for him. He's gone crazy, that one, renovatin' churches and buildin' fancy new rectories up and down the coast." The pastors nod their heads and one says, "I'm embarrassed to get up in the pulpit on Sunday. How can I be askin' my people for money, me livin' in my fancy new house and them barely gettin' by? I didn't want it, and I told him so, but he wouldn't listen." The others mumble their assent. I nod my head with them, hoping Flynn will notice.

After dinner, Jim and I walk out on the porch. The sun has disappeared except for a glowing rim on the distant hills to the east. Jim pats his stomach. "Boy, Mac, that was good!"

"Well, my soon-to-be-deacons." We turn around to see the Bishop and Gerry Cox, his chancellor. Both are dressed in black suits and clerical collars. The bishop wears a large gold cross around his neck. He smiles and shakes hands. "What do you think of this place?"

"It's beautiful," Jim says. Bishop Maher cocks his head toward me. "And you, Greg, how are you doing?" He has a fatherly smile.

"Actually, Bishop there is something that's been bothering me."

"Oh?" His forehead creases slightly.

"I mean, I know we don't take an actual *vow* of poverty, but I'm having trouble reconciling the *spirit* of poverty with your building program." I want to confess to him, to have him understand my dilemma. I want him to spiritually reassure me.

"Greg, you don't understand anything!" His face is suddenly flushed, his lips pinched. "We have to show the people of Santa Rosa that the Catholic Church is not a fly-by-night institution." He thrusts his pectoral cross in front of my face, "It's here to stay!" He sweeps his arm toward the dining room. "That's why I bought this house. Do you know who my neighbors are?" He spins me around and points down the hill, naming off bank presidents, winery owners, judges.

I hold up my hands. "Okay, Bishop, okay."

Breathing hard, he centers his cross on his chest, then turns abruptly away. Monsignor Cox glances at Jim, shrugs his big shoulders, and follows him out. Jim shakes his head. "Jeez, Mac, you seem to have found Leo's hot button."

Back at the seminary I have a recurrent dream. I'm walking in a long, narrow ditch that gradually gets deeper and deeper. I can't get out of it. Then it morphs into a grave. I wake up breathing hard, with a heavy feeling of dread inside. I see the early morning twilight filling the tall window frame across from my bed. A breeze rustles the orange trees in the courtyard below. Three months, that's all I've got. Then I have to take the vow of celibacy and become a deacon. Is that what the ditch is all about? How can I take such a vow? How can I promise to be celibate, or anything else, for the rest of my life when I've changed so radically in the last two years? I picture myself as a young seminarian, full of fervor and certitude. Then a kaleidoscope flickers across the screen: Bergson, Honest to God, Mississippi, the movie. I am no longer that innocent young seminarian. I'm not sure who I am or who I might become.

A couple of weeks later I'm typing a theology paper

at my desk when there's a knock at the door. Monsignor Cox is standing there like a big bear.

"Hi Greg. Can I come in? I need to talk to you."

My heart speeds up. "Sure."

He looks around the sparse room, then goes over and sits on the bed. I settle back down on my wooden desk chair.

He hunches over and rubs his hands together. "Well, the bishop wanted me to come down and talk to you." He straightens his back. "I mean, he's heard stories about all the radical stuff you've been doing down here, and before he ordains you a deacon he wants me to ask you," he shrugs his big shoulders, "do you really want to be a priest?"

I sit back in my chair and blow out a breath. "That's a good question." I swallow. "And I don't have a clear answer for you. I do feel called to the priesthood. It's just ... " I pick up my pen and twirl it between my fingers, "I don't know if I'll fit in. No one in the seminary knows what parish life is like, and no one in the parish knows what we're thinking in the seminary." I look up at him but Gerry is hunched over again, staring at the floor. "I don't want to go out and offend all the old ladies. I guess that's why I'd like to be ordained a deacon, so I can work in the parish and see what it's like before deciding whether I want to go on to the priesthood."

Gerry's still staring at the floor, but he nods.

"I know this isn't the way it's usually done," I say, "and I'll totally understand if the bishop doesn't want to do it."

Deep down, I'm hoping he won't.

Gerry shrugs his shoulders. He takes a deep breath in and puts his hands on his knees. "What the Hell?" he tells me. "I'll see what he says."

He looks back at the floor for a minute. Then he looks at me. "You know, maybe you can explain something to me, Greg." He bites his lip. "I don't understand what's going on in the seminary these days. I mean, when I was in the seminary, shit, we went out with girls, but we knew it was wrong! Today guys go out with girls, and they don't think it's wrong! They don't even feel guilty about it! I just don't understand that attitude."

I feel the adrenaline race through me. "Damn it, Gerry. That's exactly what pisses us off – the double standard. You guys never really question anything. You just do things and then feel guilty about them and go to confession. If it's wrong, don't do it; but if it isn't wrong, then don't slink around feeling guilty about it. Just do it. That's why you don't understand what's going on in the seminary. You've never questioned anything in your life!!"

Gerry holds up his hands. "Okay, okay. Don't get mad. I get your drift."

## THE OATH OF CELIBACY

Spring comes, and baseball season. I smell the freshly cut grass and wish I wasn't so busy with seminary politics. On my way out of the refectory after lunch I spot Father Ron Chokal standing off to the side. He edges up to me and whispers "We need to talk." He's new on the faculty and I don't know him well, but I've heard good things about him from some of my younger friends who have him for philosophy. He's definitely an egghead, not as radical as I would like, but with a good, caustic sense of humor. We hang back until the others have headed off, then walk slowly along the service road.

"What the Hell did you do to Fenn?"

I look at him blankly. "What are you talking about?"

He glances behind us. "In the faculty meeting last night, he voted to clip you! He said you came up to his room and tried to tell him how to run his class."

I feel my stomach knot up. I stop and look at him. "That's what he said? That I was telling him how to run his class?"

"Yeah, he was really pissed about it." He glances around again and motions me to keep walking. "He wasn't able to get any of the other faculty to vote against you, but he was really pissed."

I stop again. "That son of a bitch! All I did was tell him his sarcasm was turning us off in class." Chokal nudges me to keep walking. "I figured he needed someone to give him some honest feedback. He didn't tell me he was upset. He thanked me for being frank."

He shakes his head. "You told Fenn he was turning you off? What, are you crazy? He doesn't care if he turns you off. All he cares about is that you shut up and memorize your textbook."

"Yeah. Well, I guess I blew that one." I look at Chokal again. He's grinning. He seems to be enjoying this. "Okay. Thanks for the heads-up." I walk away, breathing shallow breaths. Damn, I should have known! Guys like Fenn will always put the institution ahead of the individual. Hell, maybe Chokal would too.

Two weeks later, a letter arrives with Santa Rosa Diocese letterhead. It's from Gerry Cox. "The bishop has agreed to go ahead with your ordination to the deaconate."

Damn! The ball's back in my court and the racquet feels like a dead weight in my hand. I start dreaming about the ditch again. At dawn the dim light in the window mirrors my ambiguity. How can I promise celibacy and obedience to a Church in which I no longer believe? I lack the faith to be a priest. Yet who am I, if not a priest? And if I decide to leave, what about my parents? My mother has always told me it's my decision, not to worry about her. Recently, she's even started suggesting that I research other colleges

in the area, "just in case God isn't calling you to the
priesthood." Despite her words, I know it would devastate
her. And my father ... having a priest son is all he ever
wanted.

That night I walk down to the library. The reading
room is empty. I pick a volume of the *Catholic Encyclopedia*
from the reference shelf and bring it over to the heavy
wooden table. The article entitled *Celibacy of the Clergy* is
several pages long so I sit down on one of the straight-
backed chairs. The authors present celibacy as a wonderful
development, intended by God himself. Their tone bothers
me and I realize I can no longer read their words as a loyal
son of the Church. I have to read between the lines to
find the information I want: Celibacy was not mandatory
in the early Church, not until the twelfth century when
Rome started forcing celibacy on married priests, first by
disenfranchising their wives and children, then by declaring
them slaves, the property of whatever ruler would enforce
the new edict.

I make the mistake of sharing this information with a
few of my classmates. "Where do you get that stuff, Greg?"
guffaws Ken Kelzer. "You sound like Martin Luther."
Leonard Duggan shakes his head. "You're getting awfully
bitter, Mac."

A young priest from Sacramento shows up for dinner
the next Monday night and Jim Kidder pulls me aside.
"That's Arnie Miller, the new assistant pastor at my parish.
He loves history and he's so radical he's been driving the
bishop crazy." He laughs. "You'd probably like him." After

dinner Jim and Arnie are standing with a couple of other Sacramento guys. I wait for a lull in the conversation and introduce myself. "I've been reading about celibacy," I say. "Is it true it didn't become a law until the twelfth century?" Arnie looks at Kidder and the others, then looks back at me and grins. "Yeah, up until then each priest owned his own church and could deed it to his kids. By imposing celibacy, Rome got control of all the property just like that." He snaps his fingers. "The laity never wanted their priests to be celibate. They used to beg the bishops to make their priests get married so they'd stay home and stop screwing all the women in the parish." Everyone laughs. "Seriously," Arnie says.

The weeks pass and the more I think about celibacy the angrier I get. What a stupid law, just another way to ensure subservience. Stupid or not, though, it's still a requirement for the deaconate, and I need to work as a deacon to see if I want to be a priest. It's a catch-22 situation.

I wake up the next morning, relieved, with a plan. Father Fenn's recent betrayal has inspired a solution. I'll fake the vow, just the way he faked his gratitude to me. I can justify my dissemblance just as he justified his.

My hand shakes with excitement as I draw up a disclaimer stating that I do not believe in, nor intend to take, the vow of celibacy, that I consider it an unreasonable prerequisite for the priesthood. During Easter vacation, I take it down to the bank in Kentfield and have it notarized by an unsuspecting teller. The date is May 12th, 1966, a week before we're scheduled to take the oath.

On a bright Thursday morning, my class gathers outside the theology classroom, each of us clutching a Bible. I look around to see which translations my classmates have chosen. Al Larkin has a copy of the newly-translated Jerusalem Bible, favored by the liberals. Jim MacDonald is cradling the more moderate Knox translation. Leonard Duggan and Jim Kidder proudly flout their dog-eared copies of the Douay-Rheims, the official weapon of the Counter-Reformation.

"Our last hour of freedom," quips Mike Murray, and everyone laughs. I smile, but groan inwardly. Part of me is disgusted by their naive bravado, another part wishes I could share their excitement and joy. I used to be one of them, an idealistic Christian warrior ready to sacrifice everything, even my sexuality, for the cause. But now I'm an outsider, a quisling.

Father Fenn appears at the end of the hall and walks toward us with an armful of papers. He wears his usual brittle smile and I'm relieved that it doesn't change noticeably when his eyes meet mine. It's fitting that he should be the one to administer the oath. He is, after all, the champion of law versus love, discipline versus freedom. I can tell he cherishes the role as he sets the papers down on the desk and straightens the sash on his cassock. His hair is precisely parted and combed into a stiff wave. When we are all seated, he holds up the stack of papers and widens his smile. "These are copies of the oath you will repeat after me." He hands them to Leonard Duggan and he passes them around.

Still smiling, Fenn clasps his hands together and holds them in front of his chest. "Your oath today will place you in the company of an elite corps of men who have dedicated themselves to the service of God. Four years ago you received tonsure and had your hair cut as a symbol of renouncing the world. Now you will renounce the pleasures of marriage in order to be free to serve God with all your heart. It is a huge step. But you needn't be afraid. Your oath will trigger an outpouring of God's grace which will give you the courage and strength to live out your commitment."

His words bounce off me like sharp hailstones. I feel like Herbert Philbrick sitting in a Communist cell meeting. I'm an imposter, a spy. The god he speaks of is not my god. My god is calling me away from these trappings of organized religion, toward the streets, toward humanity.

He lowers his voice. "Please place your hand on the Bible and repeat the oath after me." I lower my right hand, but let it hover just above my bible so it's not actually touching it. Mike Murray is sitting directly in front of me, so Fenn doesn't have a clear view of my desk. I hold the paper in my left hand, my fingers crossed underneath to ward off any magic this ritual might possess. As my classmates repeat the oath, I silently mimic their words, watching Father Fenn to make sure he isn't looking too closely at my lips. I feel strangely at peace.

It's over very quickly and we're back outside. Jim Pulskamp rolls his eyes down at his crotch. "That wasn't so bad. I didn't feel anything." Everyone laughs, nervously trying to dismiss the gravity of what just happened. I look over at Jim and remember us running through the neighborhood together. Today, I realize, I have severed that sweet bond of childhood.

## KIDNAPPING JESUS

I'm lying face down on the floor. The carpet is coarse, so I rest my head on my right arm, sleeved in the white cotton of an alb. A thick cord is cinctured tightly around my waist. The white cotton smells of starch, the carpet of compacted dirt. Out of the corner of my eye I see Jim Pulskamp prostrate next to me. High above us the choir sings the litany of the saints, and the congregation responds *"Ora pro nobis"* after each name. The rhythmic chant dances over our humbled forms, asking angels and saints to bless our ordination as deacons. I stare at the carpet, find a speck of dust and fix my gaze on it. The words from Ash Wednesday come to mind, "Dust thou art and unto dust thou shalt return." This too is dust, this silly ceremony, all the hoopla from parents and friends, the giddiness of my classmates during the last few weeks.

Somewhere in the church my mother is kneeling, praying for me, hoping that God is truly calling me, but nevertheless fearful for her troubled son. My father is unaware of it all, confined to a hospital bed, mind and body scrambled from yet another stroke. His absence hollows my insides. This was his dream, and now for me it's reduced to a mote of dust on the carpet.

The rest of the night blurs. The bishop calling my name, the stole being placed over my shoulders, embraces by fellow clergy, then congratulations by my mother and friends. I should feel happy, and I smile to reassure them, but I'm a stranger here, viewing their excitement through the kaleidoscope of my disillusionment.

I sleep fitfully that night and wake up dreaming again about the long deep ditch. It stretches out ahead of me as far as I can see. I will walk in it forever. There is no escape.

In the morning I rub my eyes and force myself out of bed. Stop being selfish. You have a mission. I don my black suit and snap my clerical collar around my neck. It feels like a band-saw against my Adam's apple, a prisoner's shackle, but that doesn't matter. I have arranged to bring communion to my dad today, the one act that will make this whole charade palatable.

Father Red O'Connell waits for me in the sacristy holding a gold locket on a black cord. "You know what you're doing, right?" The locket is the *pyx*, used to transport the consecrated host from the tabernacle to the sickbeds of parishioners. Red hesitates before handing it to me. His nephew Jerry has warned him, I'm sure. Jerry's the president of the class ahead of me and we don't get along. He disapproves of my politics and was one of those who pushed to have the movie destroyed. O'Connell opens the sanctuary door for me, then braces his foot against it so he can watch my every move at the altar. I'm supposed to genuflect at the foot of the altar, then again at the top when I reach the tabernacle, then again after I unlock the tabernacle. It's all spelled out in the *Rubrics,* the red print in the Missal. It's a holdover from the Roman custom of bending your knee to the emperor to show your unworthiness in his presence. Jesus never wanted people to be genuflecting to him. He preached love, not rules and rubrics. I'm here to bring Jesus to my dad, not to satisfy Red's fetishes about rubrics.

I reach the bottom of the stairs and feel Red's eyes boring into me, daring me to flout tradition in some subtle way. Without genuflecting, I ascend the stairs and reach for the key in the tabernacle door. Resisting the programmed impulse to genuflect again, I unlock it and remove one of the hosts from the gold vessel inside. I place it in the *pyx* and snap it shut. Then I place the cord around my neck. Out of the corner of my eye I see Red moving full into the doorway, blocking it. I lock the tabernacle and turn to walk toward him. His face is blotched, veins stand out in his thick neck. I descend the steps and approach him, readying myself for his outburst. He opens pinched lips and is about to speak when his eyes fall upon the gold *pyx* hanging from my neck. We both realize it at the same time: he is forbidden by canon law to speak to anyone carrying the consecrated host. We stare at each other for a long moment. Then he moves aside and lets me by. As I reach my car, I look down at the *pyx* and feel like I have just executed a heroic rescue.

When I get to the hospital, I tuck the *pyx* into the breast pocket of my jacket. I was here two days ago, visiting my dad, dressed in my regular clothes. Today I say hello to the same nurses and orderlies. This time, however, they don't recognize me. Their eyes get as far as my collar and they bark "'Morning, Father; 'Morning Father." It's a gauntlet of robots. Will this be my lot from now on? Will no one ever see me as a person, only as a Roman collar?

My dad sits slumped in his wheelchair, strapped in with a wide fabric belt. He looks up at me and raises one eyebrow. "I'm here to bring you communion, Dad." He nods and smiles vaguely, so I take out the small stole I have in my pocket and put it around my neck. Then I open the *pyx* and remove the host. "The body of Christ," I say, holding it up. He automatically extends his tongue, the way he has done since childhood, and I place the host on it. After he's swallowed it, I offer him a glass of water. "You're probably wondering why I'm dressed like this," I say. His eyebrow goes back up. "Last night I was ordained a deacon. That's the last step before becoming a priest. But … " and here I'm trying to be very careful, remembering how ecstatic he was nine years ago when I first entered the seminary. "But I'm not positive I'm going to be a priest."

He looks straight at me, his pale grey eyes showing just the slightest twinkle. Then he shocks me.

"You'll never be a priest," he says, shaking his head.

"Why?" I blurt. "Because I'm so much like you?"

"Yep," he says. The twinkle fades, replaced by his usual faraway smile.

## LIFE IN THE RECTORY

My mother doesn't believe me when I come home and tell her what happened. "Oh you're imagining things," she says. "He hasn't been that coherent in years. Plus he'd never say something like that. All he ever wanted was to have his son become a priest."

Three days later I report to St. Rose Church to begin my summer assignment as a deacon. Monsignor Tappe ushers me into his spacious study and gestures to a soft leather chair. The carpet is thick and the walls are lined with dark teak bookshelves. This elegant study is one of the crown jewels in Bishop Maher's building program. I squirm in my chair, trying to imagine Jesus sitting there, his bare, calloused feet soiling that virgin carpet. Monsignor grins at me through a set of bright dentures and clacks them as he sweeps off his glasses and points a gnarled finger at me. "Gregory! The trouble with young priests today is," he knits his eyebrows and squints, "they have lost the spirit of Poverty!" He spits out this last word, bouncing it across the plush carpet into my disbelieving brain.

The Monsignor prides himself on being a scholar and a preacher, and for the next twenty minutes he spares me none of his pedantic fervor. Finally he pushes his chair back and says, "They tell me you are a bright lad. I went to the bishop and I said, 'Send me Gregory, Bishop. I'll straighten him out.'" He clacks his grinning dentures. "You will have two preaching assignments this summer, and I am also appointing you as chaplain to the Legion of Mary. Your room is the white one down the hall." Still grinning, he stands up. "Welcome to St. Rose." Clack!

Oh no! Not the Legion of Mary! That's a paramilitary prayer group that claims the Virgin Mary as their commander-in-chief. I immediately conjure up a gaggle of fervent babushkas who will accuse me of heresy and tattle on me to the monsignor.

The Legion meets on Tuesday night in the church basement and I'm a few minutes late for their next meeting. Five grey-haired women are sitting at a table listening to a dark-haired younger man read from some kind of manual. They all look up as I enter, and the man comes over and shakes my hand.

"Welcome, Father. I'm Everett Leary. We're so glad you're here. Our praesidium has been without a chaplain for some time."

"I'm just a deacon. You don't have to call me *Father*. Greg is fine."

The ladies come swarming up. "Oh Father, so nice to meet you. Will you be leading us in the rosary tonight?"

"Uh, sure." I'm hesitating because, even though I said the rosary every night with my family and also during my early years in the seminary, I haven't said it for a couple of years now and I'm not sure I can even remember the mysteries. Luckily, tonight is the sorrowful mysteries, and they were always my favorite, so I manage to stumble through.

Mal Costa's resonant laugh fills the dining room the next morning as we share a late breakfast and trade stories about Monsignor Tappe. Mal shares many of my liberal views and, unlike the other priests in the parish, seems to understand my misgivings about the Church. He pours fresh coffee into his cup. "How did the Legion meeting go last night?"

"Actually," I say through a mouthful of toast, "I was surprised. I thought Monsignor was setting me up with a bunch of reactionaries, but those people are really friendly. I liked Everett a lot."

"Everett's our resident saint," says Mal. "His wife thinks he should have been a monk."

That afternoon my phone rings, rousing me from a nap. I pad across the thick white carpet and pick it up. "Hello?"

"Father McAllister? This is Bridget at the reception desk. You have a letter here." Her voice is pleasant, friendly.

"Thanks, Bridget. I'll be right up."

Two bright blue eyes meet mine as I enter the reception area. She tilts her head and smiles as she hands me the letter. Dark curls frame Irish freckles. "I hear you met my uncle Everett last night."

"Oh, is Everett your uncle?" I reply. "Nice guy." My heart is beating a little faster than usual. "My name's Greg, by the way. You don't have to call me Father. In fact I'd prefer you didn't."

"Okay," she says. "It's just that Monsignor made a big deal about us calling you Father, but you know how old-fashioned he is. I'll call you Greg."

Back in my room, I feel strangely exhilarated. What a nice person! And so mature for a high school student. That night I dream about her. I wake up and notice my penis is stiff. I masturbate slowly, thinking of Bridget's eyes, her hair. I no longer believe it's a sin to masturbate. I'm beyond that now. I think back to the anatomical dummy in our biology classroom. Where would my stiff penis go, I wonder, if I was in bed with Bridget right now?

The next morning Monsignor Tappe storms into breakfast muttering something about "that woman!" Mal looks up from his eggs. "What happened, Monsignor?"

"That Helen Herrold! She comes to early Mass every morning and, as soon as I get up to preach the homily, she sits back and puts her feet up on the kneeler. Then she opens up that conservative rag *The Wanderer* and starts reading it right in front of me!" He shakes his head and clacks his teeth. "It's disrespect, pure and simple. The trouble with the laity today is they've lost their respect for the clergy!"

Mal is looking down at his plate, trying not to laugh.

"Who's Helen Herrold?" I ask.

"Helen Herrold is a thorn in my side," thunders Monsignor.

"She's quite a character," says Mal. "She converted to Catholicism from the Church of England and was hoping to stay in the nineteenth century. She's not very happy about all the new changes."

"The British have never learned respect," clacks Monsignor.

A week later Mal invites me up to his room for a drink. Two other priests who live in the rectory are there as well, sitting in the old armchairs Mal has collected over the years from parishioners. "Make yourself a drink," he says pointing to a low hutch with several bottles. The scotch is already open, so I pour from that.

"How are you liking St. Rose?" asks Jim Gaffey, a boyish-looking history scholar who teaches at the local Catholic high school and lives at St. Rose.

"I'm enjoying it more than I thought I would."

He frowns. "More than you thought you would? So you were thinking you wouldn't like it here?"

"No, not that. I was just worried that I wouldn't fit into parish life. I have a lot of questions about things."

"Like what?" Gaffey demands. I can see I've ruffled his conservative feathers.

Mal breaks in. "Speaking of questions, I got this letter today from Joe Herrold." He holds up an envelope and turns to me. "You remember Monsignor talking about Helen this morning? Joe's her son." He takes a letter out of the envelope. "He's down at San Jose State studying music and he says here that he'll only return to the Catholic Church if I can answer these questions for him when he comes home for vacation next week." He holds the letter under the lamp and reads. "Number one. I have heard that the blood of St. Januarius changes from 74 degrees to 98.6 degrees every year on his feast day. Is this true?"

Everyone laughs. "He's as crazy as his mother," says Gaffey.

Mal chuckles and hands the letter to me. "I think this is something right down your alley, Greg." I look at the list of questions. All of them refer to obscure saints and bizarre reports of miracles. All but the last. Number ten simply says, "What about birth control?"

"He snuck that last one in, didn't he?" I say.

Mal smiles and nods. "Probably doesn't want his mother to know."

"Okay, what the heck. Send him my way." I stuff the letter in my pocket.

Joe shows up a few days later wearing a wrinkled sports coat and scuffed shoes. I greet him at the door and, before I can introduce myself, he says, "Where's Father Costa? Did he get my questions?"

"Yes, he asked me to meet with you. My name's Greg" He glances around as though he's expecting an ambush. I lead him into one of the small office cubicles down the hall.

"Joe, I don't know that I can help you much," I say, spreading out his letter on the desk. "As far as all these miracles you're asking about, I have no idea if they're true or not. But you know the Church doesn't insist you believe them."

He nods and runs his fingers through tousled hair.

"As far as birth control goes, well, there's a lot of

controversy about that." His eyes lock onto mine. "But personally I think it should be up to each person's own conscience."

Joe looks at me blankly for a minute, then nods his head and stands to shake my hand. "Thank you."

We're all in Mal's room that evening when the phone rings. He picks it up and listens intently for a few moments before he speaks. "Helen ... Helen ... " He shakes his head and removes the phone from his ear. He holds it toward us. A strident gabble echoes across the room. Pointing toward his desk Mal gestures for me to pick up the other phone. I ease it from the cradle and put it to my ear. "That Father McAllister has ruined my son! I'm not giving another cent to your church! In fact, I'm tearing up my envelopes right now! I don't ever want to see you again! And I hope you get sick from those figs I brought you!"

She finally runs out of breath and Mal injects his warm, calm voice. "All right, Helen. I understand. I want you to come in tomorrow at ten o'clock and we'll talk about it." Surprisingly, Helen stops yelling and agrees.

Mal hangs up, shaking with laughter. "The figs!" he chortles. "Helen and her figs!"

I'm laughing too, but I'm also mortified. "See," I say. "This is just what I was afraid would happen, that I'd come to the parish and get everyone all upset."

"Don't worry," Mal says. "Helen's bark is worse than her bite. You'll be able to calm her down."

"Me? I thought you were going to talk to her."

"No, this is a good pastoral opportunity for you." The

others laugh, though I notice Gaffey doesn't laugh as hard as the others.

"She's liable to end up in the mental hospital after talking with me," I say.

The next day Helen arrives at 10 sharp and Mal politely tells her that he's asked me to talk to her. She purses her lips and glares in my direction, but says nothing. I lead her down to the same cubicle where I talked to her son.

"Have a seat, Helen." I go around and sit on the other side of the desk, hoping it will offer some protection if she lunges for my throat.

"Helen, I understand you're upset with me."

She jerks her head to one side and fixes her glare on the wall. "I don't know what's happened to the Church today," she blurts in a clipped British accent. "It used to be you'd ask a priest something and he'd give you an answer. Now all they ever say is "I don't know, I don't know, I don't know.""

The sing-song *I don't knows* stand out from the rest of her machine gun monologue. "Every priest I meet these days, all he can say is 'I don't know, I don't know, I don't know.' No one knows anything!! Except Father Persano. He's the only one I respect. Now don't get me wrong. I don't like him. But I do respect him." Helen is still talking to the wall, seemingly oblivious to my presence. "One time in the confessional I was confessing my sins, and I kept repeating the same sin over and over again, I guess I was being a little scrupulous, and he finally yelled at me – right in the confessional, he yelled, 'Helen, shut up!!'

right there in that confessional." She pauses for a quick breath. "Well I was very angry at him for that. In fact, I was so angry, the next day when he was in church saying his breviary, I sneaked up behind him and yelled in his ear, *'I hope you die in mortal sin and go to Hell!'* I was that mad at him. But all the same, I respect him, because he didn't just say, 'I don't know, I don't know, I don't know.'"

Helen still hasn't looked at me and she's spitting words like a Gatling gun, giving no indication that she'll ever stop.

I take a deep breath and pause. Then, at the top of my lungs, I yell, "HELEN, SHUT UP!!!"

She turns and looks at me with wild, terrified eyes. A long second passes as we hold each other's stare. Then, simultaneously, we both burst out laughing.

We walk out of the office arm in arm, still laughing, and I catch a quick glimpse of Monsignor peering out his study door at us. Later that week, Helen invites me over to her house and shows me her fig tree.

## THE ROMAN COLLAR AS WEAPON

I park my car in the garage behind the rectory, but walk around to the front door so I can pass the reception desk. Maybe Bridget will be there and we can talk. The other day she said, "You'll make a good priest. You're not stiff like Father Gaffey or snotty like Father Clark. You're more like Father Costa."

I like her. We seem to have a lot in common. She's rebelling against the nuns in her high school just the way I'm rebelling against the seminary faculty. It's fun to talk to her. She's not at the desk today though, and the regular receptionist, Mrs. Reilly, beckons to me as I come in. "Father, Monsignor would like to see you in his study."

Monsignor is seated behind his massive desk, his hands tented over his nose. He clacks his teeth and gestures me into the leather chair.

"Gregory, your sermon yesterday. It was a good first effort. Clear delivery, good audience contact." He pulls off his glasses and lowers his eyebrows. "But your theology needs work, Gregory. You quoted the Beatles three times and the Bible only once. Who is this 'nowhere man' you were talking about, and what does he have to do with the

Gospel?"

Luckily Bridget is working that night and she laughs when I tell her about Monsignor's critique. "Oh my God!" she says. "He gives the most boring sermons in the world. Everybody loved your sermon."

Later that week I return from my hospital visits and see Mrs. Reilly waving me toward her desk. "I'm so glad you're here. Father Costa was called to the hospital, and there's no one else to take calls." She rips a phone message out of her register. "This woman sounded quite upset. She just hung up, so you might still be able to reach her." She jams the message into my hand. "She called from the jail."

I dial the number as soon as I get to my room. A gruff female voice answers. "Tier two, Sergeant Mullins speaking."

"This is Father McAllister from St. Rose. Could I possibly speak to ... " I glance at the paper, "Maria Jenkins?"

"Hang on. She's just headed back to her cell, but I'll see if I can catch her."

A moment later a strained voice comes on the phone. "Hello?"

"Maria, this is Father McAllister from St. Rose's."

"Oh, Father, thank you so much. I didn't know who else to call. It happened so fast. The sheriff came and arrested me and ... " she chokes back tears, "took my children away."

"Why Maria? Why did they arrest you?"

"I'm not sure. They said I defrauded welfare, that I had gotten money from my husband. But that's not true. They made a mistake. My kids were so scared! Please help me, Father. I have no one else to turn to."

"I'll come and see you right away. Just try to calm down and we'll see if we can straighten this out. How do I find you."

"I'm on the second floor, on the women's side."

"Okay, I'll be right over." I pull out my black suit and Roman collar. The more armor the better.

The desk sergeant is pudgy and has a deep southern accent. I flash back to the Mississippi jailor who laughed when I objected to him using a cattle prod on Black prisoners. "Why? They's animals, ain't they?"

I try to look relaxed, professional. "Father McAllister to see Maria Jenkins."

The sergeant sweeps his eyes over my black suit and collar. "Sure, Father. Have a seat. I'll page the women's side." The collar starts to feel good around my neck, a badge among badges.

Ten minutes later a squat female jailor opens the door and ushers a small Hispanic woman into the cubicle where I've been waiting. She is attractive despite her disheveled hair, puffy eyes, and the dull grey jumpsuit that hides her figure. She gives me a firm handshake and sits down across from me. Then she waits for the jailor to move outside the door.

"This is crazy," she says. "My husband and I separated two years ago. He moved out of town and I haven't heard from him since. He's never visited the kids or sent us any money." She brushes dark hair out of her eyes. "I guess he moved back to Santa Rosa a few months ago without telling us, and then he got arrested last week. My social worker just assumed we'd gotten back together and that I hadn't told Welfare about it. She never talked to me about it. She just sent the sheriff to arrest us."

Monsignor had warned me that St. Rose was a magnet for con artists, and that I should refer any beggars to the St. Vincent de Paul Society. But Maria wasn't a beggar. And she didn't seem like a con artist.

"Okay, Maria. I'll go see the kids, and then I'll check out the rest of your story. If you're telling me the truth, I'll do everything I can to help. What's your husband's name?"

"John. John Jenkins."

"And he's in this same jail?"

"Yeah, I guess. Over on the men's side."

"Okay, who else should I talk to? Do you have any relatives or friends that could vouch for you?"

She gives me two names, one of them her brother.

"My brother won't be much help. Ever since he got rich, he will hardly talk to me."

I head over to the men's side and again use my collar to wrangle an interview with John Jenkins. He's got a brawler's physique, but he hangs his head when I tell him about my conversation with Maria.

"No, Father, she's right. I never called her. I feel really bad about that." He looks down at calloused hands. 'I really should've contacted them when I first got back. But, you know, I was workin' a lot of overtime at the trailer factory."

Maria's two little girls are being held in the county

foster center. They approach me warily behind a sour-looking nurse, the older holding her little sister's hand. "Your mommy's going to be back very soon," I say. "You just have to be brave for a little while, then you'll be back home." Looking into their tear-filled eyes, I wish I could take them back to the rectory with me. Even Monsignor would be less scary than this slack-jawed nurse who now hustles them back into lock-up.

Maria's brother has a real estate office downtown. He wears a silk tie and starched white shirt and his dark hair is carefully parted. "My sister, she's no good, Father. She's never been any good. Got married to that jerk when she was way too young, and never made anything of herself." He adjusts the glass paperweight on his desk. "I hate to say it, but that's the way it is. She's just a bad seed."

On my way out to Maria's house, I stop by the trailer factory where John worked. His boss has a patina of wood dust on his hair and shirt and chews a big lump of gum as we talk. "Yea, John's been here ... what? ... three months? He installs custom interiors for me. He's a good solid employee. No problem at all. 'Til he got himself arrested, of course."

The other name Maria gave me is Bob Franklin. He rents a room in the back of her house and answers the door with a dishtowel over his shoulder. "I've known her and the kids for a long time, Father. She's a great person, a wonderful mother. I'm an old friend of John's, but I can tell you, he really blew it. He took off and left her and the kids without a dime." He tosses the towel back at a chair.

"I stayed, because, you know, the rent's good and I like the kids, and I figured I could help her around the house. As far as this fraud charge, she had no idea John was back in town. Neither did I."

The next morning, I call the welfare office and ask who is in charge of her case. They give me the name of her social worker.

"No, I mean who will be hearing the case?"

"Oh, Judge Murphy. He hears all the fraud cases."

The judge's secretary is bristly until I identify myself. Even then she is hesitant to schedule an appointment for me. I project my new-found collar power over the phone. "This is urgent, Ma'am. Mrs. Jenkins is a parishioner of mine and I am very concerned that her case may have been mishandled." I'm betting Murphy is a Catholic. "I'll have to take this to Bishop Maher if I can't get in to see the judge today."

"All right. How about three o'clock this afternoon?"

I arrive fifteen minutes early. The secretary offers me a chair and busies herself at her desk, avoiding eye contact. At exactly three, she knocks on the judge's door and ushers me into his chambers. The dark bookshelves are almost as opulent as Monsignor's. The judge is behind a long oak desk. Sitting across from him is a woman festooned in a bright yellow sun hat. Her dress and scarf, also shades of yellow, are stylish and expensive, though definitely eclipsed by the hat. The judge's robe is hung on a clothes tree behind his desk. He wears a drab blue shirt and striped tie. His grey hair is closely cropped. He rises as I come in.

"Good afternoon, Father. I've taken the liberty of inviting Mrs. Piltorch to our meeting. She is Maria's social worker."

I reach out to shake her hand. She raises it as though she expects me to kiss it.

"Now then," the judge says, motioning me to a chair. "I understand you have some concerns about the case."

"Yes, your honor. I've spoken to Mrs. Jenkins and researched her case and I'm convinced she has been falsely accused." Mrs. Piltorch presses her lips together and jerks her head. The brim of her hat flaps.

I begin reading from my notes, summarizing each interview. Piltorch interrupts once to correct a minor detail. I notice her voice is shaky.

I finish and Judge Murphy glances quickly at Mrs. Piltorch, then back at me. "Well certainly, Father, you're not so naïve as to believe that that man Franklin would be living at her house and they wouldn't be sleeping together." Piltorch is nodding earnestly.

I summon my collar voice. "Your honor, as I understand it, the way you play the game – in terms of the law – people are innocent until proven guilty. And I've seen no proof that he is sleeping with her. The way I play the game – in terms of morality – I don't see as how that matters. What matters is that she and her kids shouldn't be in jail."

The judge is glaring, his face now as red as hers. He stands abruptly. "Thank you for your input, Father. I'll take it under consideration."

"Thank you, Your Honor. Nice to meet you Mrs.

Piltorch. "This time she doesn't offer me her hand.

I drive back to the rectory gripping the steering wheel to control my anger. Self-righteous bastards!

After dinner I tell Mal about my encounter with the judge. "It's that same old self-righteous crap," I say "It doesn't matter whether it's the Church or the legal system. It's all the same."

The phone rings. He answers and hands it to me.

"Father, it's Maria. The kids and I are home. The judge ordered me released a couple of hours ago. I just can't thank you enough."

Back in my room, I look around at the freshly painted walls, the comfortable furniture, the plush carpet. Then I think of Maria and her kids. I have it so easy here – three meals a day, a car at my disposal, no family obligations. *Blessed are the poor in spirit.* This is a trap.

I look up to Heaven. "I'm willing to be a priest, Lord, but this doesn't feel right. Here I am, sitting in the lap of luxury without having paid my dues. Let me experience the bottom. Then maybe I'll feel worthy to be a priest."

## DECISION

Two weeks later I'm back home, scratching my head. I am no clearer now than I was six weeks ago about becoming a priest. Working as a deacon didn't help. Everyone I met at St. Rose said I would make a great priest. I didn't destroy anyone's faith while I was there, and no one thought I was a heretic, except Father Gaffey.

But do I want to do it? A sheet of paper is on the desk in front of me. I've drawn a line down the middle and written *Pro* over one column, *Con* over the other. The sides are even. I'm stuck. I can't decide. In one more week, I'll have to go back to the seminary. Part of me dreads going back, but at the same time I can't conceive of myself as anything but a priest. As long as I can remember, people have treated me like a priest. Who would I be if I wasn't a priest?

I awake early the next morning in the midst of a dream. I'm hearing a familiar voice in the dream. The voice has authority. "Greg, you really want out. It's okay. Just leave." It's the same voice that spoke to me nine years ago, telling me to take the test for the seminary. It's Jesus, still calling me to his priesthood, but now sending me away from the organized Church.

Relief floods my body. It's true, I *do* want to leave, but I want to carry the priesthood with me. Is that possible? My torso tingles, blood rushing through veins long constricted by some deep-drawn corset. I taste the clear water of an open future and it intoxicates me. Energy surges up and down my spine linking gonads to brain, brain to gonads. Bridget flashes into my mind. I must tell Bridget. I must tell them all, but most of all Bridget.

My mother is slicing oranges in the kitchen when I walk in. Two places are set on the grey formica table. "Good morning!," she says.

"I've decided," I say. "I'm leaving."

She nods, puts the knife down, and wipes her hands on the dish towel. Then she sits down. She stares at the table for several seconds. "What will you do?" she asks softly.

"I'm not sure. Get a job."

"Mm. Where will you live?"

"The city probably. I'm not sure yet."

She takes a deep breath. "Well, it's good you decided now, instead of later. What about school?"

"I don't know, Mom! I just now decided."

Tears appear in her eyes and she dabs at them with her napkin. "Yes, I know. Excuse me." She gets up and goes into the bathroom. I hear the water running. She comes back in and sits down again, but the tears persist. She forces a smile. "I'm afraid this is going to take a while to sink in. I think I'll call your aunt Agnes and see if I can go up to her place for a few days. That'll give you some space to get organized."

I feel nauseous. Yes, she always told me this was my decision, that I shouldn't make it for her or for anyone else. But I always knew, deep down, that my leaving would devastate her.

She sits quietly for a while, then gets up and puts the dishes in the sink. "I'm proud of you," she says. "I know it took courage." She gives me a gentle kiss on the cheek, then goes into her bedroom to pack.

I call Mal Costa and tell him what I've decided. "What's the protocol for telling the Bishop?" I ask.

"You better call Monsignor first. He's fond of you, even though he doesn't always show it. Ask him to tell the Bishop and arrange a meeting. And you better let your pastor know."

I think of Red O'Connell glaring at me from the sacristy door. "He'll be glad to hear it."

Later I sit at the small wooden desk where I used to do my homework as a kid. My room hasn't changed much, same bed, same bureau and nightstand. I'm the one who is different, poised for some blind adventure that fills me with excitement I haven't felt since childhood. I glance out the window where the creek used to run under the street. I remember the first time I felt these stirrings. Jim, Tony and I were sitting on the moist sand under the old bridge, two wooden matches from my Grandfather's smoking can stashed in my shirt pocket. I had a copy of the Independent Journal, still folded in the tight V that made it easy for the paper boy to throw. I unfolded it and crumpled a few pages into a ball on the wet sandbar. The shallow creek eddied past us. A car rumbled across the bridge overhead, and Tony scrambled out into the sunshine to look up the road. "It's only Mr. Waldbillig," he said, squatting down again. I took out a match, held it between my thumb and forefinger and flicked my wrist toward the flat rock in my lap. The match snapped in two. "No," Tony said, picking up the broken match and holding his forefinger near the head. "My brother showed me. You have to put your finger against it so it doesn't break." I took the second match out of my pocket, held it like he said and pulled it firmly along the rock. Flame burst orange and red. My genitals flew up in my stomach. I touched the burning match to the edge of the paper and watched the fire greedily eat the newsprint. Jim and Tony stared at it too, mesmerized. The paper flared and rolled into blackened ash along the wet sand. Tingling with excitement, I felt my penis grow hard, thrilled by the illicit power, the possibility. It's the same feeling as now, sitting at my desk about to write these letters declaring my new identity: A free man, a rebel against authority, a radical follower of Jesus. Bridget dances across my mind, and I pen the first letter to her. After that I write to several of my classmates, remembering how bad I felt when other seminary friends left without telling me. Late in the afternoon I walk up the street to Jim's house and find him practicing the piano in the living room.

"I've decided to leave, Jim."

He swivels around on the piano bench and nods slowly. "Well Mac, I can't say I'm surprised, but I'm sorry to hear it." It's a priestly response, masking, I think, the discomfort he's often felt about my radical ideas. Even so, we both know that this will shatter the camaraderie we've enjoyed since childhood. We're both sad, even if a little relieved.

I write to my parishioners at St. Rose, to friends of the family, even to my godmother in Idaho. I want them to grieve my parting, feel the drama of this moment, Shane riding into the sunset.

Monsignor arranges an appointment for me with the Bishop. Is that relief I see on his face? "We're sorry to lose you Greg, but I'm sure you've prayed about this long and hard."

"Yes, Bishop, I have."

"What are you planning to do?"

"Well, I have to find a job and then … "

"Good!" He jabs a finger at me. "That's just what you need. Your problem is you think too much. You need to get a job."

"Well, I'm also planning to go to school, maybe San Francisco State."

He frowns and shakes his head. "I don't think that's a good idea, Greg. Now that you've left the seminary you'll probably become interested in young women – after your dispensation from Rome, of course. But I don't think you'll find any suitable young women at San Francisco State. Now Lone Mountain College, there are a lot of fine young Catholic women there, and it's very important to find someone who shares your interests. For instance, if a young woman likes opera."

Opera? What's he thinking? "Actually, Bishop, I don't know anything about opera."

"Well you know what I mean. If not opera, something else having to do with art and culture."

Good Lord! This from a guy who never reads anything but stock market reports and the sports page. "Thanks, Bishop. I'll keep that in mind. And thanks for sticking with me through all this."

"You're welcome, Greg. Good luck." He stands and extends his gold-ringed hand.

I shake it, but I don't kiss his ring.

PART TWO:

# THE SORROWFUL MYSTERIES

## THE HAIGHT & S.F. STATE

The fog creeps over Twin Peaks as I drive my '59 bug from our apartment in the Haight-Ashbury to St. Paul's Church. My roommates are still sleeping off the pot Craig turned us on to last night. Two years ago, Craig almost got thrown out of the seminary for getting drunk at a pizza parlor and missing dinner. The faculty grounded him, so he got back at them by riding his bike around campus on holidays, singing Beatles songs at the top of his lungs.

I still feel a slight buzz as I drive past St. Joseph's Hospital where I was born 26 years ago. Chris and I dug the pot. Ringer said he preferred scotch. Mike took only a token puff, because he had promised his cheerleader fiancée at Cal he wouldn't touch the stuff. The church parking lot is packed, but I squeeze the bug into a corner slot and half-walk, half-jog toward the soaring gothic entrance. My heart is beating fast as I slide into a rear pew. It's been almost a year since I've been in a church, and it feels cold, strange. The scent of incense and the glow of candles that once comforted me, now feel like symbols of oppression. It could be me up there, waiting with my robed classmates to walk down the stone aisle. Instead I'm getting a Master's degree in Creative Arts Interdisciplinary Studies at San Francisco State and living down the street from the Grateful Dead. The organ thunders a prelude. Everyone rises and turns toward the rear as the choir breaks into song. I watch the hierarchy of males stream up the center aisle, first the well-scrubbed, pink-cheeked altar boys carrying candles and a tall crucifix; then a phalanx of seminarians, dripping propriety and symmetry; then my classmates, the honored ones, dressed in white albs, some smiling and looking around, others with downcast, pious eyes. After them, a long column of priests of every age and shape, many giving officious nods to their friends in the pews. Next come the bishops in their red robes, miters perched on balding, white-haired heads. Finally the Archbishop himself enters, holding his staff in his left hand, blessing the crowd with his right.

The organ thunders on, and I wonder what my old classmates would think of my life now, what they would say to my roommates, how they would act in my graduate seminars. Last week we had to go around the room and describe our Master's projects. Ralph said he was experimenting with noise – "John Cage, that kind of stuff." Everyone except for me seemed to know who John Cage was. A chubby woman with chopped blonde hair gave each of us her Nazi psychologist look and said, "I intend to use Esalen encounter techniques to liberate creativity." Everyone waited for her to say something else, and when she didn't, Fred, an ex-monk in a dashiki finally said "Far out! That sounds great. I plan to explore Herman

Hesse's bead game." I know who Hesse is, I've even read <u>Siddhartha</u>, but I've never heard of any bead game. When it was my turn, I looked around at the nine other faces, so passionate about art, music, witchcraft, psychotherapy. "I'm not sure yet," I told them, "but I think I want to write something about God, humor and creativity." They all gave me blank looks. Finally dashiki Fred said, "Far Out."

The procession has now reached the altar, and the choir intones the litany of saints. My classmates prostrate themselves on the sanctuary floor before the Archbishop. I wonder if they're distracted by the dust motes on the carpet as I was. Stroking my new beard, I imagine what Jesus would think of all the pomp at the altar. He probably would have run most of these guys out of the temple and then gone out to hang with the prostitutes and sinners. My mind wanders to Suzanna, sitting at the edge of the circle in my graduate seminar, her pale blue eyes framed by delicate lines, dark hair spilling over her bare shoulders. She has her tanned legs crossed, a sandal dangling from her bare foot. "I'm a dancer," she says in that feathery voice. "And I'm working with the bio-energetic theories of Wilhelm Reich and Fritz Perls." I can't take my eyes off of her. She intrigues and scares me.

The woman sitting next to me in the pew pulls a lace handkerchief out of her purse and wipes her eyes. My classmates are still lying prostrate. When I gave Suzanna a ride home from class, she said, "I'm performing this weekend. Do you want to come?"

On the altar the bishops sit stiffly in their chairs, and I think about Suzanna and those two male dancers, performing totally nude in a little warehouse studio. Her lithe body slithered in and out of theirs like a snake. Is Suzanna the kind of woman Bishop Maher warned me about? After the dance performance, she gave me a copy of Wilhelm Reich's The Murder of Christ. According to Reich, Jesus was sexually free, uncontaminated by the *emotional plague* that afflicts humankind and chokes off the basic (sexual) energy of life. They killed him because they found His freedom too threatening.

My classmates stand in line before the Archbishop, pledging him their obedience. I imagine myself up there between Len Duggan and Jim MacDonald, my mom sitting in the front pew watching her perfect priest son ordained. Only a year ago I was standing on the altar with Jim Pulskamp, wearing the same white alb. Now I go to anti-war marches and hang out with a nude dancer who thinks they killed Jesus because he was sexually liberated. It's a different brand of priesthood. The woman next to me dabs her eyes again. She has no idea she's sitting next to a guerilla priest who was called by Jesus away from organized religion. The woman looks over at me and smiles. Her lace collar and dainty gloves remind me of my grandmother. I smile back.

At the ceremony's end, I sit with my eyes closed and listen to the voices and laughter echoing through the cathedral. Parents, relatives and friends are pushing their way to the altar where the newly ordained will give their first priestly blessings. What was that scripture line about *make no man your master*? I open my eyes and get up to stand in line, just another member of the laity waiting for a blessing.

Len Duggan's narrow shoulders are hunched as he lays his hands on the head of the blushing nun ahead of me. He leans down to whisper priestly words in her ear. He's good at wooing nuns. When she steps aside and I move up, his face darkens momentarily, then he smiles. "Hey, Mac, glad you could make it. I almost didn't recognize you." He seems uncertain about what to do next, so I go down on one knee. "Okay, Leonard, lay it on me." He puts his hand on my head. I feel his fingers trembling slightly. He murmurs the blessing. When it's over, I stand up and stick out my hand. "Congratulations." I say. He looks at my hand a minute before he shakes it. "I'm not contagious," I want to tell him, but I go on to the next line, wondering if my friendship with Leonard can survive his priesthood.

When I've received all the blessings I can handle, I duck out the side door and stand on the stone steps in the glaring sunlight. There's a quick, fresh breeze in the air. I can still feel the imprint of all those hands on my head, hear the echoes of all those blessings. As I walk toward the parking lot, I have the strange feeling that I might have to break into a run.

# 31

## PANTHERS, PICKETS & PRIESTS

The Black Panthers visit the California Legislature in May, nattily clad in their black leather jackets and berets. They listen to the proceedings for a while, then, at a signal from Huey Newton, pull out rifles and handguns, legal firearms at the time. No more police brutality against Blacks, they shout. We will fight fire with fire. It's a declaration of war, one they are destined to lose. I admire their courage, understand their rage, identify with their challenge to arrogant authority. My own life seems dull in comparison, a regular daily ritual similar to the seminary: Classes in the morning, then over to the student center for lunch and whatever political rally is scheduled that day. Strident activists strut back and forth, bull-horning us like revival preachers, thundering invective. I'm usually sympathetic to their cause, but something about their pinched brows and lack of humor keeps me from answering their altar calls. Around two thirty, I don my Park & Rec jacket and head to my job as a playground director.

War has just broken out between Israel and its Arab neighbors. Suzanna's eyes are puffy when I pick her up for lunch. "I'm terrified. I haven't been able to sleep ever since the shooting started," she says. "I've decided to move back to New York to be near my family. I'm leaving next week." She already seems far away. Will I ever see her again? God, I wish we'd slept together.

San Francisco State is immersed in its own war. As I walk into the auditorium to register for next semester's classes, I see a phalanx of cops standing outside the administration building. They're wearing black jumpsuits, eagerly stroking long batons. When I come back out, the cops are still there, along with several TV camera crews and a large crowd of students. A helicopter beats ominous rhythms overhead. "What's going on?" I ask a longhaired guy in an army jacket. "Sit in," he answers, "to protest the administration giving student information to draft boards."

I arrive at Rochambeau playground ten minutes late. Buzzy Bozzini is pulling baseballs and bats out of the equipment closet when I walk in. I drop my backpack on the desk. "Sorry Buzzy, I ran into some delays at school." She sucks in her lip and raises her eyebrows. "Okay, get this stuff into the duffle bag for practice." She walks over to the door and looks out at the tennis court. "Hey Kennedy!" she yells, "that better not be a cigarette in your hand!" Buzzy's a tough little broad from North Beach, who terrifies all the teenagers at Rochambeau and has a reputation for scaring off her assistants. "So what was so important that you had to take last Saturday off?" She's got her hands on her hips, chewing a wad of gum, still eyeballing the playground.

"I went to see my classmates ordained. I used to be in

the seminary."

When I look up, Buzzy has the first smile on her face I've seen since I started six months ago. "Yeah?" she says, "You studied to be a priest? My best friend at Presentation High became a nun. She left me her gym shoes when she went into the convent. I still have 'em."

At home, I unlock the door and find a pile of mail under the slot. There's a letter from Bridget. I toss my roommates' mail on the living room table and go into the old dining room I have converted to a bedroom. It's stark, like my room in the seminary, just a desk and a bed, though this bed is a double bed, testament to fantasies yet unrealized. I sit on the soft mattress and stare at the letter. My heart speeds up as I tear open that sticky flap where her tongue was. In her bubbly handwriting she says, "I can't wait to be done with high school. I've decided to move to the city this summer and get a job." My stomach flutters. My hand moves across the mattress feeling the space where no girl has ever slept. I lie back on the bed and look up at the old chandelier. I think about Bridget's visit over Easter vacation, how on Good Friday we danced all night to The Grateful Dead at the Fillmore Auditorium. Bridget wove in and out of the strobe lights, her eyes reflecting the psychedelic light show that filled the screen behind the stage. Then that night, driving home, it had gone wrong somehow. I was telling her about an anti-war rally, and I felt her turn away from me. She was on the edge of her seat, her hands under her legs, looking out at the city rushing by.

"My dad was shot down over Poland in World War II." Her voice was quiet and hard. "So don't expect me to agree with you about the war." The car was suddenly cold, and remained so until I dropped her off at her sister's apartment. I didn't try to kiss her goodnight, even when she thanked me and gave me a hug. We spent the next day together, but now I was more cautious, holding back.

My own father is still at the Rafael Convalescent Hospital. I push his wheelchair around the grounds, filling him in on my life. He shows little response to my stories, but I notice the little smile whenever I try to be funny. Back in his room, I straighten his robe, adjust the pillows and restraining strap on his chair, and start to put on my jacket to leave. He slumps in his chair, his soft eyes vacant. Suddenly his head jerks upwards. His eyes turn feral and an angry snarl escapes through bared teeth. I jump up and run over to him. "What's the matter, Dad? Do you hurt somewhere?" He jerks his head toward the open door behind him. "Rahrrrr!" I look past him into the hall. A small man in a red baseball cap is laboriously wheeling himself past the door, his toothless mouth twisted into a grimace, hollow cheeks bristling with unruly whiskers. As he inches along, he glances, wide-eyed, into our room. My dad still has his back to the door, but he continues snarling until the man disappears down the hall. Then he looks back at me and flashes a sheepish, conspiratorial grin.

I stop at my mom's for dinner that night. She's washing lettuce at the sink while I pour bourbon and soda over ice. "Has Dad ever growled when you visit him?" I ask.

"Oh yes," she laughs, "there's one little fellow that just sets him off. Your father starts snarling every time he comes near."

"But the guy was out in the hall," I tell her. "Dad had his back to the door. I don't think there's any way he could have seen him."

"I don't know what it is." She wipes her hands on a towel. "It's like he has radar. Or maybe he can smell him. It's strange though. Your father never behaves that way around anyone else. Only when that strange little man comes around."

"Do you suppose the stroke unleashed some sort of werewolf strain in him?"

"Oh for pity sake! You and your harebrained ideas!"

Back in my room, I sit at my desk, composing the prayers of petition Jim Pulskamp asked me to read at his first Mass. I'm determined to make them meaningful and provocative, not the usual pious pap. Bridget's letter lies at the corner of the desk, taunting me. Soon she'll be here in the city, and what then?

*Let us pray for Father Jim, that he have the courage to remain honest and open, even in the face of pressure and criticism.* After Mass, I stand near the back of the parish hall sipping a cup of coffee and watching the parishioners file in to congratulate Jim. I nod to some of them. A year ago they would have come over and talked to me, but now they don't know what to say, so they just wave and head toward the reception line where Mrs. Pulskamp stands next to Jim in her blue dress and matching pillbox hat and veil. She smiles and dabs her eyes as she greets the guests. Finally, her dream has come true. I see Jim's older brother Bill standing off to one side with his wife and two boys. Years ago, he entered the seminary, then left after only a year. His decision to leave devastated his mother. Now she's weeping for joy, but he looks relieved as he puts his hand around the small son hugging his leg. My mother stands behind a table, pouring coffee and tea for the guests. Periodically I see her glance over at Mrs. Pulskamp and force a smile.

---

## BRIDGET

---

Bridget moves to San Francisco that summer and, despite my reservations, I begin spending a lot of time with her. In August, I hitchhike across the U.S., sleeping along deserted freeways north of Cheyenne, jumping freight trains in Duluth, crashing in roach-infested flophouses in Chicago. All along the way, I send Bridget letters detailing my adventures. At night, she begins to take Suzanna's place in my dreams.

Just after I return there's a shootout in East Oakland. Huey Newton, one of the founders of the Black Panthers, is accused of killing a policeman. The Panthers claim it was self-defense in a police ambush, the police claim it was murder. San Francisco State is simmering with unrest when I return for classes in the fall. The anti-war protests have morphed into demands for increased minority enrollment and more Black Studies courses. There is talk of a student strike.

Leaving the Haight on my way to the annual Park and Rec staff meeting, I notice "Free Huey" signs plastered everywhere. There's a revolution brewing in this city, though you couldn't tell it from the Park Department. I look around the room at the crew cuts, clean-shaven faces, and shiny coaching jackets. I'm the outsider here, the only one with a beard, my faded director's patch safety-pinned to my old blue sweatshirt. I sit down next to a ruddy-faced guy wearing a Giant's baseball cap.

"Jim Chumley," he says, holding out his hand, "Larson Park." Larson's a little one-person playground out in the Sunset District. "I got my Rec degree from City College two years ago," he says. "Subbed for a while then got my own playground. You a Rec major?"

I smile at him. "Nope. Philosophy."

The supervisor hands out the new assignments. I'm relieved to get a regular Sunday/Monday assignment at a place with a gym. That means I won't lose hours when it rains. Chumley looks down at my sheet. "Upper Noe! Oh man, that's out in the Mission District. I subbed there a couple times. It's a tough place."

On Monday afternoon I drive out to Upper Noe Playground. I park my car just off Sanchez Street in front of a cement wall that has *fuck you* spray-painted in black letters. A bunch of teenagers are standing on the sidewalk. They watch me as I walk toward them along the high cyclone fence surrounding the playground. I pass between them to unlock the gate. "How ya doin'?" I say. Some nod slightly, most just stare at their cigarettes. I walk through the gate past tennis courts and a baseball field. The building to my right is an auditorium connected to a vaulted gym that extends out in an L-shape. Buzzy told me the park is about 20 years old, built back in the '50s when this was a working-class neighborhood made up of Irish and Italian Catholics. "Most of 'em didn't stick around to enjoy it," she said. "They all moved to the Sunset and Richmond districts as soon as the Mexicans started moving in." Now the neighborhood is home to the Day Street gang, mostly young Chicanos, along with a few leftover Irish and Italian brawlers. They all grew up at the playground and still consider it home. I open the door to the breezeway separating the gym and the auditorium, and unlock the Director's office. It's strategically located, with windows on three sides so that I can see the auditorium, the fields and the gym. Kids begin to filter into the gym and I soon hear the thud of basketballs and the squeak of sneakers. I'm sitting at the desk filling out my time sheet when a couple dressed like Roy Rogers and Dale Evans appears at the office door. The woman's hair is dyed bright yellow under her white Stetson and heavy rouge makes her cheeks look like rubber balls. "I'm the dance instructor," she snaps. "I need you to unlock the auditorium." We go into the auditorium and I watch her cowboy friend set up a portable phonograph while she sorts through a pile of 45 records. "I hope you can keep those hooligans from disrupting my class tonight," she says. "This is the worst venue in the whole city." She glances over at the window where two kids are peering in. "I've had several of my dancers refuse to set foot in this place ever again." She looks over to the door as several adults sidle in, looking like frightened refugees from a dude ranch. They quickly close the door. "Did you have any problems out there?"

she asks. "No worse than usual," shrugs a guy in a fringed Western shirt. "Just had to run the smokers' gauntlet."

I go back and check the gym, and have just returned to the office when I hear the scratchy sounds of fiddles and accordions, accompanied by a shrill female voice. "Swing your partner . ." Kids start appearing from nowhere, drawn to the auditorium like rats to the pied piper. Soon they're on the roof, jumping up and down in time to the music, yelling obscenities at the windows, banging on the doors. I charge out of the office and they scatter like roaches, but as soon as I turn around they're back again. I don't know any of their names, and I can't see them in the dark anyway. Pretty soon the auditorium door flies open and Dale Evans is standing there shrieking into the darkness. "Stop it, you hoodlums! Stop it!"

The next week I see a police car pull up in front of the park. Two cops jump out and push their way into the milling circle of teenagers. I pull on my Director's sweatshirt and head out toward the gate. "What's going on?"

A curly-haired cop has his back to me, holding one of the kids by the jacket collar. His hands are big and square. He turns his head toward me and his eyes lock first on my beard then sweep down to the director's badge on my sweatshirt. "We got a complaint that these punks were fighting and disturbing the peace," he says.

The kid shakes his head. "Man, here we go again." The cop cuffs him with his free hand. "Shut up!"

I look at the cop's badge. It says O'Reilly. I extend my

hand. "Greg McAllister. I'm the Monday night director."
He isn't about to let go of the kid and take my hand.
I smile at him and shake my head. "I've been here all
evening, and I haven't seen any fights. These guys were just
standing around smoking and bullshitting as usual." The
cop looks at me hard under bushy eyebrows. The kid starts
to pull away, but he jerks him back. "You know how it is,"
I say. "Some of the old-timers around here think there's a
riot every time three teenagers show up together on the
sidewalk."

One of the Chicanos laughs and the other cop says,
"Shut up, Lopez!"

O'Reilly lets go of the kid. He looks over at his
partner, then back at me. "Okay." He straightens up and
tucks his shirt into his pants. "Just make sure these creeps
keep the noise down. I don't want any more calls tonight,
understand?"

I'm barely back in my office when there's a knock on the
door. I look over and see a stocky kid with curly dark hair
sticking out under a blue stocking cap. I recognize him as
one of the guys who are always smoking out front. Several
of the bigger guys are standing behind him. I motion him
in. He opens the door and takes a step inside. "Hey man,
what's your name?" he says in a clipped Mexican accent.

"Greg."

"All right, Greg. I'm Carlos."

"Glad to meet you, Carlos."

"Man, I just want to thank you for backing off the pigs
out there. Most directors, man, they just take the cops' side

no matter what."

"Well, you weren't doing anything wrong. If you were, I would've taken their side."

Carlos nods. "Okay. Well, thanks again, man, I mean, Greg." He rejoins the group and they saunter back toward the sidewalk. As they pass my window a few of them nod to me. From then on, no one disrupts the square dance lessons.

A year later, Carlos will cajole me into accompanying a busload of neighborhood kids on a camping trip to Yosemite. "It's a Youth for Service grant, Greg. If we can't find a chaperone, we won't be able to go, and a lot of these kids have never left the Mission District. It's a really big deal for them." Against even my fuzzy-liberal judgment, I agree, and then watch helplessly as Carlos and thirty of his inebriated homeboys terrorize family-friendly Yosemite Park for a weekend. It's like unleashing the Hells Angels on a church social.

"What do you think?" says Bridget picking up Craig's copy of The Berkeley Barb from our coffee table. A picture of Huey Newton dominates the front page. "Are they setting him up or did he really do it?"

"Probably both," I say. I'm glad she's interested, questioning things more. Ever since she left home and moved to the city, she's gotten much more radical. She's even agreed to go to the anti-war rally in the park this weekend. She kicks off her shoes and leans back on the sofa, folding her legs under her dress.

"How's life at the phone company?" I ask her.

"I'm getting fast," she says, reaching for the bulky San Francisco White Pages. "Give me a name."

"Try mine," Ringer says from his chair in the corner. He's sipping Scotch and reading the newspaper. "James Ringrose the third."

She fans the upper right corner of the phone book, leafing rapidly through the pages. "Here you are."

Ringer tweaks his moustache. "Quite impressive, young lady."

I look over at Bridget. She flashes her blue eyes at me. Why haven't we ever slept together? We've been dating for three months now, but we've never had sex. What's hanging me up? At first I worried she was too young. But now she's eighteen, living on her own. Am I still waiting for Suzanna to come back? That's stupid, she probably isn't interested in me anyway. No, it's just fear. I'm still a cowardly celibate.

After dinner, we sit and drink Red Mountain wine out of jelly jars. We talk about her work, my work, the Black Panthers. Then I can't stand it any longer.

"Why don't you stay here tonight? You don't have to work tomorrow."

She smiles. "Do you have a shirt I could wear as a nightgown?"

She comes to bed in my blue denim work shirt. I gently unbutton it, run my hand lightly over her breasts. I feel a tingling in my fingers, then in the rest of my body. We sink into the pure pleasure of it. Easier than I thought.

## DEATH

I stand at the foot of the hospital bed and watch my dad's pale blue eyes vacantly meander until they meet mine, then go soft with recognition and love. They resume their vague odyssey around the room until a sudden stab of pain turns them into the eyes of a bewildered little boy, astonished that anyone would want to hurt him. My tears seem to bewilder him all the more.

"It could be hours," the doctor says, "or even days."

"You need to go." My mom touches my hand. "Go do your Park and Rec interview. Nothing's going to happen right away. You can get over and back in a couple of hours."

I have to show up for this interview if I want to be granted permanent status. I look at my dad. Up until now the stroke was benevolent, merely depriving him of his mental functions. It never caused him physical pain. Now I'm watching him flinch under some invisible scourge.

Our next-door neighbor Liz puts her arm around me. "You can't do much good here. If he sees you crying, it might make him feel worse. Go to the interview. It'll be fine."

Part of me welcomes her absolution. I lean over and

kiss my dad's thin cheek. "I'll be back, Daddy."

The interview is ridiculous, an empty formality, a fatuous nod from the jocks of the Park & Rec Department. How could I get sucked in by another stupid bureaucracy? Why didn't I stay with my dad? The Golden Gate Bridge blurs past my window as I race back toward the Marin hills. I swing into the hospital parking lot, rush past nurses and orderlies. My dad's door is open. I run in. The bed is empty, flat with fresh sheets, tightly tucked. At the nurses' station I find my mother and Liz filling out papers. My mother's eyes are bloodshot. She gropes in her purse and pulls out a linen hanky. "Oh, Sweetheart." She wipes tears from her eyes. Liz puts her arm around her shoulder. "About twenty minutes after you left," tears well up again and she presses the hanky into them, "your dad died."

Our family has always used Keaton's, the Catholic mortuary. I've read Jessica Mitford's book on the funeral industry, so when the mortician starts showing us $5000 caskets, I stop him and ask for time alone with my mother. We sit on an ornate metal bench surrounded by gleaming caskets with velvet linings. I take her hand in mine. "Ma, this guy's trying to guilt-trip us into buying an expensive casket. That's not what Dad would want. He'd want to keep it simple."

There's a viewing and rosary the next evening. I smell the sweet odor of tired flowers and see familiar faces from the neighborhood and from church. My dad inspired so much love in these people. He never accomplished great things in the world, but he brought warmth and humor to these people's lives, and they remember. I hear Bob Hambly talking to Sally Neal through smiling tears. "Mac was the only one who could get Mayme Kennedy to laugh. She usually didn't get the joke, but she'd laugh anyway just because Mac was telling it. He snuck some pretty good ones past her." I look across the room at my dad's profile in the plain wooden coffin, the large nose my grandmother assumed was Jewish when she first saw him. Is he listening to all these stories? Does he know how much I love him? I look down at my hands and see his long tapered fingers. I hope I can bring people the same joy he did. People are talking softly, hushed by the canned organ music that permeates the room. I walk down the hall and find the mortician sitting behind a large oak desk. His dark hair is meticulously combed and he's wearing the requisite black suit and sanctimonious smile.

"Yes?" he says, rising from his chair.

"Is it possible to turn off that music?" I ask.

"Are you sure?" he says. "People usually like a little organ music in the background."

I want to punch him. "Yes. I'm sure. My dad was a very witty guy and all these people want to remember him that way. That music is a downer."

"Well, there is a certain decorum that we need to maintain," he says.

I glare at him. "Please turn it off!"

At the end of the night, my mother and I stand over the open casket one last time. She smiles down at my dad's face, that same sweet smile I remember shining between them when I was a little boy.

"Goodnight, Sweet Prince," she says, and kisses him gently on the cheek.

## TRAPPED

The eucalyptus trees are swaying in a spring breeze as I open the office door at McCoppin Park. Frankie and his brother are waiting for the basketball as usual, and a couple of mothers are watching their kids play in the sandbox. This is very different from my last playground. There's a lot more fog here in the Sunset District, and a lot more parents than I used to see at Upper Noe. This is where all those Irish Catholics fled when the Hispanics moved into the Mission. Right across the street is the Taraval police station and from my desk I see the police van pull up and disgorge members of the Tac Squad in their black jumpsuits. They laugh and joke and poke each other with their riot batons. They looked so much more menacing an hour ago, when I faced them across the picket line at San Francisco State.

I look out at the playground where more kids have joined the basketball game. I resent these white kids, the sons of patriotic police and firemen. They have no idea what's going on around them, Martin Luther King assassinated in April, Robert Kennedy in June, napalm in Vietnam, Reagan screwing up California. And under all of it, the gaping hole in my heart, the absence of my dad.

My hand reaches out to the phone, but then I draw it back. I see my mother's blushing face at dinner that Sunday night, the way her eyes darted before she finally asked the question. "Are you and Bridget … sleeping together?"

Her frankness had disarmed me. "Yeah, we are."

She was biting down hard on her lip. "Next thing I know you'll be calling me up telling me she's pregnant."

"For God's sakes, Ma, give me a break. What do you think I am, really stupid?

I reach out for the phone again. Damn her! Bridget promised me she was taking care of the birth control stuff. She even got testy when I brought it up. "Never mind," she said, "it's all under control."

Well it's not under control. Neither am I. I feel like I'm back in that ditch again, stuck in someone else's mold. And now I have to deal with my mother.

I dial and then sit there, looking out at the basketball court where Frankie and Jack are playing Horse. The phone rings twice, three times.

"Hello?" My mother's voice is cheery and vibrant.

"Hi Ma. We, uh … Bridget just found out that she's … pregnant."

"Oh Lord, I knew it! Well I hope you're satisfied." She slams down the phone. I lower the receiver, take my head in my hands. "I … hate … this."

Two minutes later the phone rings. Her voice is calmer now, measured. "All right. We better talk. Come over for dinner."

All the way across the bridge, I keep hearing Bridget's words from the night before. "The test came back positive. I know you don't believe in marriage, but I'm going to have this baby anyway." I can feel my stomach getting queasy again. Coils tighten around my body. I can't walk away from this. I'm trapped. Again. Inside Waldo tunnel I scream at the top of my voice until I'm hoarse and breathless.

My mother and I face each other across the kitchen table. Dinner is finished, our empty plates pushed away. She swirls the ice cubes around the watery remnants of a highball. Her lips are pursed, her blue eyes fixed on the table in front of her. "I thought you were planning to go to Europe next year."

"I was."

"Are you going to marry her?"

"Well I can't just walk away from my own kid.

"Can you and Bridget *get* married, in the Church I mean, when she's … you know?"

"Knocked up?"

"No, I didn't say that."

We back off and sit in silence. She runs her fingernail along the placemat and shakes her head slowly. "I don't know how you can stand before God and justify fornication."

I slam my hand on the table. "God doesn't give a damn about any of that stuff. He just wants people to love each other. And not make judgments.

She gives out a little yelp. Tears begin to flow down her

cheeks. "I don't know why you have to do this to me," she sobs. "Why you have to desecrate every single thing I have ever held sacred."

Fear and guilt fog my mind. I want to reach out and console this woman who has endured so much. But then I feel a cold, righteous anger wash over me, a shield between me and my weeping mother, deflecting her tears and judgments. I turn, heartless, toward her.

"You know, Ma, all my life you've taught me to be a good Christian — to care about other people. And you've always practiced what you preached. But right now, right here, you don't seem to realize that ... this isn't the easiest thing *I've* ever gone through!"

Her head jerks up as though from a slap. She stares at me for a moment. She nods her head, tentatively at first, then more deliberately. "You're right," she says. "I'm being very selfish." She wipes her eyes with her napkin. "I'm sorry. I won't do that again."

A week later Bridget and I drive to Santa Rosa to see her parents. "This is not going to be fun," I say.

Her blue eyes are set. "Stop worrying. They'll just have to deal with reality." It's awkward as I sit down in the living room across from her father. The last time I came here for dinner, I was a deacon at St. Rose.

He looks at me over his glasses. "What are you planning to do?"

I take a deep breath. "We're going to get married, give it our best shot."

"Okay," he says. "That's good. Let me know what you

need." He goes back to reading the paper.

I walk into the kitchen. Bridget's mother is standing in front of the stove stirring something in a pot.

"Hi Barbara."

She stares at the pot. "Hello," she sighs, not looking up. She resumes stirring. Then she sighs again, like somebody's just died.

The little mission chapel in Marshall is just off Highway 1 overlooking Tomales Bay. Our small caravan of cars turns into the grassy parking area and wedding guests get out, tucking in shirts and adjusting dresses. Two priests in Roman collars walk over and the guests gather around them. "Ah, it's a lovely day for a wedding," the older one says in a clipped British accent. Father Jack is Bridget's uncle, a monsignor from Yorkshire and an old hand at this kind of awkward Catholic event. Jim Pulskamp, the other priest, sidles up to me and whispers out of the corner of his mouth, "Mac, you don't even believe this stuff anymore. How am I supposed to do this?"

I gaze straight ahead. "Just do it."

Jim and the Monsignor lead us across the lawn toward the chapel. They reach the front door and jump back quickly. The people behind them look up and gasp. A huge mass of bees is swarming over the church door. The Monsignor laughs and walks around the side, beckoning people to follow. We enter the church through a narrow back door.

## ÉLAN VITAL

I make my way up the stairs to our third-floor apartment at the corner of 24th and Dolores and catch a whiff of curry. Moisture from the soup pot has condensed on our kitchen windows. I've grown comfortable, I realize, with the daily routines of home and hearth. Bridget is in the bedroom sorting hand-me-down baby clothes. "Look at this," she says, holding up a tiny sweater. "Isn't it adorable?"

"I got a teaching job," I say brightly. "Part time at Sacred Heart. I'll still be able to keep my Park and Rec job after school."

"That's good." She lies back on the bed next to the pile of clothes and rests her hands on her stomach. Her brown maternity smock bunches up between her breasts and her stomach. "Lots of kicking today at work."

"They want me to start next week. Seventh and eighth grade."

She pushes herself up from the bed. "That's great." She pulls her black curls off her face. "I'll get dinner ready."

I open the back door and climb the rickety stairs to the roof. From there I can see the fog rolling down from Twin Peaks, enshrouding me in grey. It's all in motion.

Everything's constantly moving.

8 a.m. Monday morning I drive through the Fillmore District on my way to Sacred Heart Grammar School. After World War II, the Fillmore was a thriving center of Black entertainment and commerce, but in 1948, the politicians labeled it *blight* and targeted the area for redevelopment. Now, twenty years later, the neighborhood is in shambles. Scores of old Victorian houses have been razed, drugs and violence are at an all-time high, and the school drop-out rate is soaring. Sacred Heart is one of the few good schools in the area and the only all-Black Catholic school in the city. I lock my car and cross the sidewalk to the main doors. Through the basement window I see Black Panthers in their berets and leather jackets dishing up scrambled eggs and pouring hot chocolate for neighborhood kids. I mount a flight of well-worn stairs and walk down a polished hallway to room 2A.

Forty students in blue and grey uniforms nervously glance at me as I enter, then return their gaze to a black-clad figure. "This is Mr. McAllister," the nun says. "He will teach you English and reading in the morning and I will teach you mathematics and religion in the afternoon." Sister Miriam's stern voice rivets them to their chairs. "I don't want any of you giving Mr. McAllister any trouble, understand?" They all nod. She turns and walks out the door.

The students look at me with wide innocent eyes. Someone in back mumbles something. The girl in front of her puts her hand to her mouth and laughs. The rivets are starting to work loose. "You go'n' make us diagram sentences?" asks a fat kid in the back row. The girl who laughed puts up her hand. "You married?"

At recess that first day, I sit on a hard bench and watch James, the dullest kid in the class, unveil a hidden talent on the basketball court. Despite his tight-fitting school uniform and hard leather shoes, he gracefully fakes and dribbles around his classmates and effortlessly swishes a fade-away jump shot. As I clap for him, a young nun hurries across the playground. "Emergency phone call, Mr. McAllister." She hands me a piece of paper. "Evidently your wife is going into labor."

Bridget is already prepped when I get to French hospital. A young orderly hands me gloves, smock and mask, and leads me to her bedside. "How did you get here?" I ask.

She grins. "The bus. I came in for my regular checkup, and my water broke just as I was walking in the door."

Four hours later a delicate little creature slides out of the birth canal and begins exploring the air with tiny limbs. As I had hoped, it's a girl. She fits perfectly the name we've already chosen for her, *Élan Vital*.

I hold her in my hands, very tentatively at first. She's so light. And she's totally bald. Her eyes open and lock into mine: "Didn't think you wanted me, eh? Nice try." The nurse takes her back and places her on Bridget's chest. She eagerly hunts down the nipple and begins sucking.

Later I wander up to the nursery where the babies are displayed. Élan is the smallest one, dwarfed by Tucker, in the basinet next to her. His sign reads *13 lbs, 1 oz. Circumcise.*

Oh my God! We forgot about circumcision! Did we ever make a final decision? I rush back toward the maternity ward. Halfway there I remember she's a girl.

---

## LAURA

---

It's been a depressing winter, cold and foggy, no end in sight for the Vietnam War, or even the strike at San Francisco State. Teaching feels like an albatross around my neck, as does marriage. I resent Bridget's bourgeois domesticity, her failure to lose weight after her pregnancy. At night I hear her muted sobs next to me and feel ashamed for the coldness I feel toward her.

"Laura needs a place to stay," she says one evening. I turn from the dishpan and see her trying to wipe the spaghetti sauce off Élan's mouth. Élan squirms in her high-chair. "I told her she could stay with us for a while."

Laura is Bridget's twin sister. I first met her at St. Rose when I was a deacon and mistook her for Bridget. Now I can tell the difference. She's slightly thinner and much more outspoken than Bridget, though they're definitely from the same egg. Last year she and her politically ambitious boyfriend worked for Robert Kennedy's presidential campaign, but the assassination triggered a radical change in Laura. In the course of two weeks, she dumped the boyfriend, moved to San Francisco, and became a volunteer for the Black Panther newspaper.

"At least she's over that liberal Democrat bullshit," I say. "That used to drive me crazy." Actually, it was her boyfriend who drove me crazy. He had his sights set on a career in politics and consequently had no personal convictions about anything. Laura, at least, would always give me a good argument, and I liked that about her. "I suppose I'd be okay with that."

Bridget removes the safety pin from between her teeth and fastens a clean diaper around Élan. "Well Laura never does anything halfway, so get ready for an earful."

Just after Laura moves in, J. Edgar Hoover announces that the Black Panthers are the greatest threat to the internal security of the United States. He vows that 1969 will be the last year of their existence. Every night Laura brings home stories about Cointelpro's latest attacks on the Panthers. She also brings home lots of Panther beaus, dour, black-jacketed figures who usually arrive late and leave before dawn. One afternoon I'm sitting at my desk working on my thesis when I see a hooded figure outlined at the front door. Laura sees him too and rushes toward the door. I hear heavy footsteps thundering down the stairwell. "Asshole!" yells Laura.

She's fuming when she comes back in. "Who was that?" I ask. She yanks her fingers through dark curls. "A fucking undercover cop," she says. "Everyone's under surveillance right now, including us. Have you noticed the little click on the phone when you pick it up?" I go over to the phone and hold it to my ear. After about three seconds, I hear a distinct click. "Wow!" I say. "Let's make up some stuff and send them on a wild goose chase."

"Just be careful what you talk about," she says. She's not smiling.

In early December, the Chicago police and FBI raid a local Panther office and murder Fred Hampton in his bed. That Sunday afternoon, the phone rings. It's for Laura. I see her face go tense. She's already reaching for her coat as she hangs up. "There's going to be a raid on the Panther office. They want as many people down there as possible, right away." Fifteen minutes later she and Bridget and I are on the sidewalk in front of the Panther office along with several hundred other people. Élan is in my arms, and I swell with pride as people in the mainly Black crowd smile at her tiny raised fist. "Right on, little sister." More people keep arriving and soon we're shoulder to shoulder on the sidewalk. A city bus swings into the bus stop in front of the office. There's a loud hiss of air brakes and the door ratchets open. A uniformed driver jumps out, donning his black beret as he merges into the crowd. We stand vigil for another half hour until the leaders receive assurance from the same City Hall mole that previously alerted them. "The raid's been aborted," shouts a slender woman in a black leather jacket and Afro. "Thank you all."

We walk back toward where we parked. As I start to unlock the VW bus, I notice the butterfly window is shattered. The glove compartment is open, its contents scattered on the floor below. "Damn!" says Laura. "I'm missing my purse. I must have left it on the seat." I shake my head. "Serves us right. Honky liberals."

That night, I'm at my desk, downing a shot of bourbon when Laura comes in carrying Élan. She looks down at the typewriter. "What's the title of your thesis again?"

"*Creativity, Playful Response to Infinity.* It's about laughing through God's eyes. It's what keeps me from taking any of this shit seriously." Laura nods and smiles. In the last few weeks she and I have become allies. In many ways, I feel more drawn to her than to Bridget. She's more adventuresome, less conventional, though they certainly share the same violent temper. I never know which one of them is going to explode first. It's crazy for an only child to be living with identical twins. I have no experience of siblings, let alone what it's like to share an egg. I look over at Élan, her head resting on Laura's shoulder. Is she confused too? Does she have trouble keeping her mothers straight?

"I have to finish this thing and hand it in," I say. "I got an offer to teach Communications at Lone Mountain College if I can get my degree by this fall. The strike has delayed everything. Even the teachers are behind."

"Only the ones who were on the picket line," she says. "The scabs are probably all caught up." She heads into the living room, then turns around. "Oh, I missed your radio show this morning. How did it go?"

"Man, it was a zoo. First I had a Jesuit from Santa Clara talking about the reforms of the Vatican Council, then two gay guys talking about gay liberation. The Jesuit, he's one of these real liberal types, so he sticks around to hear what the gay guys have to say. After they've talked for a while, he can't resist. He jumps in and says, 'You know, the Church used to condemn homosexuality as a sin, but now we realize that's totally wrong. It's not a sin, it's just an illness. We need to treat it with the same compassion we'd treat any other illness.' Man, you should have heard the gay guys. They ripped him up one side and down the other. 'Father, you can take your Vatican Council and shove it up your ass.'"

Laura laughs. "Sounds like when the Panthers preach to me about women's liberation. They think they're so enlightened, but they're total chauvinists. They're still treating their women like dirt." I look at Élan. Does she have any idea what a turbulent world she's been born into?

## WOMEN'S LIB

Spring arrives. Bridget and I vow that we won't spend another summer in the fog. We begin looking at houses in Marin County. "I think that's a very wise decision," my mother says, clearing dinner dishes from the table. "It's the only way you'll ever save any money. I might even lend you the down payment, as long as you don't buy some old shack."

"Your mother!" Bridget says on our way back home. "She can never say anything nice without putting in her little dig."

"You should have met my grandmother," I say.

I check the mailbox on our way into the apartment and find a letter from San Francisco State. I rip it open and find a form letter from the Creative Arts Department.

*Dear Student, This is to inform you that your thesis/creative work has/has not been accepted. You are scheduled to meet with your graduate advisor on Monday March 12th.*

Someone has circled *thesis* and *has not.* "What the shit? I can't believe this."

"What's the matter?" Bridget takes the letter from my hand and reads it. "What does that mean?"

"I don't know. It looks like they rejected my thesis. I'll find out Monday."

Dr. Reynertson is sitting at her desk when I walk in. She looks more stern today, her auburn hair pulled into a tight bun rather than flowing chaotically over her shoulders. "About your thesis," she says, gesturing me to a chair. "The committee had no choice but to reject it. You failed to follow Turabian's citation style."

"Turabian? I thought this was a Creative Arts department. Since when are we English majors?"

She looks at me over her wire-rimmed glasses. "You're the one who chose to do a thesis rather than a creative work. If you choose to do a thesis, you have to follow the format for a thesis."

I get it now. These people probably joined the Creative Arts Department because they were sick of reading student papers. I shift in my chair. "Okay, what's the other option? What's a *creative work?*"

Her face softens. "It's two or more artistic disciplines integrated into a single presentation."

I pause for a moment. "Do you consider writing an artistic discipline?"

The frown returns to her face, as she thinks about it. "Well, yes, I suppose so."

"Good." I stand up and snatch my thesis off her desk. "In that case, I'll do a creative work."

Even my mother likes the house we've found in Fairfax. Nestled on a wooded hillside, it looks like a tiny Swiss chalet. The price tag is right, too: $18,000. Fairfax is the only affordable place left in Marin. Back in the '40s and '50s, this was where the teenagers from San Francisco would come in the summer to swim at the Marin Town and Country Club. Most of the houses, like this one, were built as un-insulated summer cottages. In the last couple of years, Fairfax has become a hippie enclave, home to the Grateful Dead and Van Morrison, along with a bevy of street hustlers, drug dealers, and paisley-eyed groupies. It feels right.

As we wait for the house deal to close, I transform my thesis into a creative work. I re-type the whole thing, leaving space for illustrations. Then I draw cartoons all over it. When I slip it under Dr. Reynertson's door, it looks more like a comic book than a thesis. Three days later, the committee approves it without reservation. The next week I sign two contracts, one to teach at Lone Mountain College and the other to buy a house.

Bridget loves the small-town atmosphere of Fairfax, as does Laura, who by now has finished her urban guerilla phase and decided to move in with us again. With her back in the house, the fearsome mysteries of twinship again confront me. Telepathic vortices of energy swirl between them and erupt into firestorms of rage that baffle my single-egg sensibilities. I become an irrelevant bystander as the two of them struggle to wrench separate identities from their common gene pool. Laura has the temporary advantage. Unencumbered by marriage, she is freer to indulge in the sexual revolution pulsing around us. "Politics has to go deeper than race and class," she declaims.

"It has to focus on gender equality and freedom!"

"Yeah, Laura," sniffs Bridget from the kitchen, "and while you're preaching women's lib, I'm washing your dirty dishes."

Laura jumps out of her chair. "Fine Bridget, be the martyr!" She storms out and slams the door. I look over at Bridget. She's glaring at the dishpan.

A few nights later, Bridget turns to me in bed. "It's not fair, you know. You get to drive off to work in San Francisco every day and I'm stuck here taking care of the house."

Uh, oh. I think I know where this is going, but I sink my foot in it anyway. "How do you figure that's unfair? I'd be glad to switch with you. Do you want to go to work and I'll stay home?"

"No, because I couldn't get as good a job as you. Men make more money in our society."

"So what do you want me to do?"

She's prepared. "I want you to do half of the housework. And I want you to take care of Élan some nights so I can have a social life."

"Do the hours I spend at work count at all in this equation?"

"No."

In a dream that night, I meet an old man dressed in rags. He looks at me, shakes his head, and speaks in a hoarse whisper: *Women's lib ... Is going to bring ... More grief to Mudville ... Than Casey ever did.*

That weekend I give Laura a ride to San Francisco.

Élan, now age two, stands behind us on the rear-facing seat of the VW bus. She's listening to Laura rant about male privilege. "Women do twice the work for half the pay. It isn't fair."

I nod my agreement, but it doesn't help. Laura's face is getting redder and she's talking louder, as though we're in an argument, even though I'm agreeing with her. Trying to lighten her mood, I say, "That's what makes them live longer."

She shoots me a withering look.

Élan sees it and leans over to whisper in my ear. "*Femis shevano pig!*"

---

## CASTLES BURNING

---

I can hear Neal Young's plaintive voice vibrating our aging windowpanes as I pull up in front of the house. Pot smoke drifts dreamily through the living room and stoned eyes glance warily up at me standing in the doorway with my bulging briefcase. I recognize Paul and Ned, a couple of vets who live down the street, and their roommate, what's-her-name. The others I don't recognize, but that's not surprising, since lately our house has become a haven for wandering stoners. No one says "Hello," not even Bridget, who merely nods at me through the haze. *"It's only castles burning,"* the loudspeaker reminds me. I step over bodies and go downstairs to the bedroom, feeling old and square for having a straight job.

Later, as we're getting ready for bed, I mention it to Bridget. "I feel like a stranger in my own house. No one even gives me the time of day."

"Oh they're all really nice," she says, "they're just shy around people they don't know."

"Well even if I didn't know someone, I think I'd have the courtesy to say Hello if I was sprawled out in their living room."

"Sure Gregory, because you're perfect." She shakes her head and walks to the bathroom.

God, I hate this. I feel like her father. I feel like everybody's father.

A few days later, I awaken to the bright morning sun glistening on the oak leaves outside my window. Élan is still in her pajamas, her head propped up on pillows. As I walk past, she looks at me over her whale book, "Where's Mom?"

"I guess she must have crashed at Paul and Ned's last night. You fell asleep around 10, so I carried you home, but your mom wanted to stay at the party. Get dressed and I'll make you some breakfast. She'll be back soon."

"Okay. Pancakes?"

The bacon grease spitting on the hot griddle reminds me of Saturday morning breakfasts when I was a kid. Henry Peck would be knocking at the back door about now, just in time for a plate of buckwheats, and my mother'd be opening the kitchen window to let the smoke out.

Élan is dressed, sitting on a stool and staring down at the small hole in the kitchen floor where Mr. Sad and Mr. Happy sometimes appear. If I stand on a chair downstairs, I can insert my index finger with a happy face, or my middle finger with a sad face. The last time we played, Élan decided to stomp on Mr. Sad with her foot.

We hear footsteps on the porch and the front door opens. "Mommy!" Élan yells, running into the living room. "Daddy's making pancakes!"

After breakfast Élan goes downstairs to play with her

dolls and Bridget sits down in the easy chair. "When I didn't come home last night did you think I spent the night with Paul?" I'm drying the last of the breakfast dishes and continue wiping a plate as I walk into the living room. Bridget is smiling at me.

"No, I just figured you got tired and crashed."

She tucks her leg beneath her. "Well I did. And it was incredible."

This doesn't fully register. "Oh," I say. Then I feel my heart crash into my solar plexus and spin off into a swirl of grey wool. I am vaguely aware of nodding and smiling, saying, "That's cool," my practiced hippie Amen to that vague dogma about exclusive relationships being bullshit and our generation being beyond petty emotions like jealousy and possessiveness. Even as I say the words I'm already plunging down a thunderous, heart-shredding tunnel at a speed that takes my breath away. "Far out," I say, as my heart explodes and shatters.

In the weeks to come, Bridget blooms, and I wither. She moves from Paul to other eager Fairfax lovers, slims down, dresses up. I thrash around our empty bed. Every glance at the post-midnight clock wracks me with jolts of jealousy. I can't concentrate at work and scold myself for being such a pansy traditionalist. On a blustery afternoon I trudge up the hill behind our house and unload into my journal about how I taught her everything I knew, urged her not to lean on me, to be herself at all costs, and now I'm feeling like a lonely old professor at the end of his career.

A few weeks later, Bridget has an appointment in San Francisco and asks me to drop her off on my way to work. She's been more available lately, not going out as much. Maybe it was just a phase, I tell myself. It's sunny on the bridge and sailboats dot the bay. I open the window to let the ocean air blow the cobwebs out of my lungs.

"You can drop me off on the other side of the park," she says. She reaches down for her embroidered handbag. "Oh, and I wanted to ask a favor. Do you think you could watch Élan Saturday night? Alex asked me to go to a concert with him."

I feel a tiny, embryonic hope miscarry in my heart. "Uh, yeah, sure. Okay."

"Thanks." She climbs out and waves goodbye as I re-enter traffic.

After work I head over to Oakland where Gene Merlin has invited me to dinner at his mother's house. Bridget used to enjoy these events, but no more. "I get bored around your old seminary buddies," she told me a few months ago. The smell of sauerbraten tickles my nostrils as I walk up to Gene's door. His mother is sitting in her overstuffed chair with her feet up. Her nylons are loose on her calves. "Where's my friend Bridget?" she demands in her German accent. "Why didn't you bring her with you?"

"Élan's sick, she had to stay home with her," I lie.

It's almost midnight when I leave. I drive over the Richmond/San Rafael Bridge, the dinner banter still rattling in my head. As I cross into Marin, I think of Bridget and feel suddenly very tired, wooed by the darkness. Wouldn't it be nice to sink into that dark?

The sound of pebbles banging off wheel wells yanks me awake. I'm doing 60 on the banked shoulder of the highway, tires spitting gravel. I pull hard on the steering wheel and the VW bus veers back into the road, tilting wildly to one side. It rights itself momentarily before listing hard to the other side. I jerk the wheel again and the bus comes back to center, but then overcompensates to the right, up on two wheels, going over, over. I hear a small voice, "Relax, just roll with it," and everything goes into slow motion, glass shattering, metal scraping. Without a seatbelt on, I roll to the right and do a slow somersault in a drawn-out cacophony of squeals and scrapings. Time comes to a halt, then very gradually returns to its normal pace. I'm lying on the ceiling of the bus. Everything is eerily quiet.

When I pull the handle of the passenger door, it swings outward, upside down. I crawl onto the pavement and hear footsteps. "You okay?" A guy in a windbreaker is looking down at me, fumbling with a flare. "I think so," I say. "I banged my left thumb, but everything else seems okay."

"You're lucky," he says. The bus is lying on its back like a turtle, wheels still spinning. I lean in to turn off the ignition and notice a dent in the roof, right where my head would have been if I hadn't rolled.

"Since you're okay," he says, "I think I'll drive into town and call the Highway Patrol. I'm hoping they'll replace my flares."

I nod and crawl over to the shoulder.

## SAD ESCAPE

The bus is totaled, but Bridget has a friend who has a used bug he sells us for $900. He's a former boyfriend, so I don't feel comfortable driving the thing. I start taking the bus to work.

Thursday afternoons are quiet on campus. I sit in my office, unable to work but afraid to go home. A woman with an armload of books passes my open door and smiles at me. I hear her unlock the office next to mine. She's sorting her books when I come to her door. "My name's Greg. I guess we're neighbors."

"I'm Lana," she says. "I'm part time, so I'm only here a couple of afternoons a week." She has tired eyes but a warm smile. Life has wrung her out but not hardened her. I search her eyes and see comfort there, perhaps wisdom. Before I know it I am laying my heart open to her, telling her about Bridget, admitting that I am not as cool about free love as I thought I was. She nods sadly. I can tell she's been there.

"If you ever need a place to stay in the city," she says, "you can always crash with me. I rent a little house here, but weekends I stay up in Bodega with friends." She seems to know what I need before I do. The next week, I take her up on her offer. We take the bus over to Church and Market and walk down a narrow sidewalk behind a Safeway supermarket. "It's a holdover from the '40s," she says, unlocking the door of a tiny cottage. It's one large room with a kitchen at one end and a desk and futon at the other. There's a small bathroom in the corner.

"This is great," I say. "How did you find it?"

"A friend lived here. When he moved, he passed it on to me." I look at her. She gives me that same tired smile. We eat dinner, talk for a while and then nestle awkwardly into chilly sheets. She reaches out and gently pulls me to her. I move my hands over her body. Her skin is rougher than Bridget's, her vagina less moist. We make love tenderly, gratefully, but without passion. That weekend I tell Bridget I'll be staying in the city with a friend on Monday and Thursday nights. She seems relieved.

"Actually, I've been wanting to talk to you about something," she says. "There's a teenager I met downtown. Her name's Jaleela and she needs a foster home."

"With us?" I say.

"She's really sweet, but she smoked some angel dust at a party last week and passed out. Now her caseworker is threatening to send her to juvie if someone won't take her. I'll be responsible for her."

Jaleela shows up the next day. She's stunning. Tall and willowy with jet black hair down to her waist, she has the aristocratic, hooked nose of an Arabian queen. She seems chronically stoned, not sloppy stoned, but like an old soul who has seen it all and is amused and slightly bored by the whole thing. I'm intrigued, and intimidated.

"I'm afraid she's out of our league," I tell Bridget. "We're way too straight for her."

"Speak for yourself," she says.

When I see Lana at school, she tells me she's going to move up to Bodega for the summer. "My place will be available if you want it."

"Oh, thanks, but I'll probably be staying in Marin."

Her patient eyes meet mine. "Okay, just in case though."

I'm feeling feverish and weak as I hand in my final grades to the registrar. By the time I get home I'm dizzy and nauseous. "You probably just need to rest," Bridget says. She's working full-time at the café downtown, so Laura and Jaleela share babysitting duties, taking Élan shopping or to the park. At night, they all go out, leaving Élan with me. It's a smooth operation. I seem to be the only dysfunctional member of the group. Why can't I shake this flu? Why do I stay awake most of the night, wondering what Bridget is doing, torturing myself with images of her, naked, in someone else's arms? Why do I feel like everyone's Calvinist grandfather?

After a week in bed, I start to feel helpless and crazy. The sunshine outside looks alien. I hear voices in the street and envy their humanness. I feel like some sort of freak, unable to adapt. One morning I awake in a sweat. I have to get out of here. These people don't care about me. I'm just an inconvenience!

Then I think of Élan. What about her? I shake my

head. You're not doing her any good right now. You're just wasting away. But I don't even have a car and I'm barely able to walk. And where can I go? Lana's house. Yes, that would work. And Dennis has a car. I get out of bed and walk to the phone, feeling less dizzy now. Even though the house is empty, I speak to Dennis in a conspiratorial whisper. "I need your help. Can you give me a ride to San Francisco?"

"Sure, I'll be there in two hours," he says. My heart is beating fast as I plot my escape. I start to feel energized. After getting dressed, I write Bridget a poem about why I have to leave and how sad I feel about that. I place it on our bed. She'll come home and find it and I'll be gone. There's power and pathos in that.

I hear Dennis drive up in front of the house. We load my bags into his Chevy sedan and we drive down the hill, past the café where Bridget works, out of my Fairfax Waterloo. When we reach the Golden Gate, the fog enshrouds me and reminds me of the sunny home I'm fleeing.

It's June and the air is cold and sodden in the city. Lana's little house feels damp and empty. I give Dennis a grateful hug and say goodbye. "I just need to lie down and cry some," I tell him.

## LSD

Two fogs, one outside my window, one in my head. Grey is all I feel. I force myself off the futon, wishing Lana was here now as I pour granola into a bowl and open the bottle of kefir I bought yesterday at the health food store when I made my resolution to change my diet along with my life. No more packaged cherry pies for breakfast.

I walk heavy-footed through the fog, down Market Street to 10th, then south toward Howard. My heart is low in my gut, seizing up every time I think of Bridget. I have to stop obsessing about her, but she hovers at the edge of my consciousness. Project One looms in the distance, a battered old four-story warehouse converted into a co-op by hippie artists and community action groups. Airwaves is constructing a community radio station in there. My therapy.

When Nixon bombed Cambodia and the students were killed at Kent State, the city went crazy and the liberal radio stations cancelled regular programming to cover the crises. Even the DJs at KSAN, the corporately owned rock and roll station, stopped playing music and started talking about politics. KSAN sponsors complained and the managers told the DJs to resume the regular format or be fired. The DJs refused and "liberated" the station in the name of the community. That lasted a couple of hours, until the managers cut the power and fired everybody. That's when a group of activists, including me, formed Airwaves, to guarantee the community a voice that couldn't be censored by corporate interests.

I reach the second floor and see Larry Bensky bending over a tub of drywall mud. His shirt and glasses are speckled with white globs. "Where is everybody?" I ask.

He smiles. "Probably still in bed." His eyes look old and there's a permanent crease in his forehead. Larry has been shepherding Airwaves ever since the Grateful Dead performed a kick-off benefit for us at the Fillmore. I look around at the bare drywall. We haven't made much progress. DJs like to talk, but they aren't much inclined toward physical labor; plus, our decision-making is seriously hobbled by a commitment to something called *consensus politics*. One paranoid naysayer is all it takes to sabotage any decision, and these days there are plenty of them.

"How are you?" says Larry. I start to answer, and he hands me a roll of drywall tape and points toward the far wall. "Can you get that seam?" Larry's the guru of radical radio in the Bay Area; he's worked at KFPA for years. I met him when I was doing Street Radio at KQED. I can't figure him out. He claims to be an atheist, is more cynic than idealist, more headstrong than heartfelt, but totally dedicated. He's certainly not someone I can talk to about my romantic woes, but nevertheless I feel comfort in his presence.

I pull the drywall knife along the tape seam, feathering the mud along the edge. I'm good for a few seams, but then the tape-loop begins rolling again, Bridget in the arms of some new lover, laughing her newfound pleasure. My hand slips and I lose my knife line. I look over at Larry. He's near the door, talking to a woman I recognize from the last meeting. She's wearing tight jeans and leans her shoulders back against the wall as she smiles up at him. Hard nipples show through a frayed Che Guevara T-shirt. Are she and Larry lovers? Am I the only loveless alien on the planet?

It's been two weeks since I left Fairfax. I miss Élan, but I can't handle going back there. I call Bridget and ask if she'll drop Élan off at my mother's house so I can spend some time with her.

"Your mother hates me," she says. "I know she blames me for everything. I don't want Élan staying there."

"Okay," I say. "We won't stay at my mom's. I'll take her up to Dennis' house in Sonoma. He's out of town this week."

Bridget's voice is cold. "I'll see if Laura can go with you."

"What? You don't trust me with my own daughter?"

"I want Laura with her."

My mother is wearing her skeptical teacher face when my friend Ralph and I pull up in his old camper truck. "I hope you're not planning to go very far in that thing," she says.

I ignore her. "Ma, this is my friend Ralph. Élan's not here yet I guess?"

"No." She's still staring at the truck, scrunching up her nose.

"It runs better than it looks," says Ralph.

"Well I hope so," my mother says. Then she softens.

"Nice to meet you, Ralph."

An old Buick pulls up behind the truck. Laura, Élan, and Jaleela get out. Jaleela's wearing a long skirt and tank top. Colorful bracelets adorn both her arms. Laura comes around and gives the driver a kiss. He pulls away. My mother looks at the three of them standing next to Ralph's truck. She shakes her head. "Humph!"

We reach Dennis' house in the late afternoon after stopping in Glen Ellen for groceries. The small living room is strewn with Dennis' books and papers. Dried herbs and strangely deformed vegetables cover the kitchen counter. Élan hovers behind Jaleela and Laura, watching Ralph and me unload the groceries. What is she thinking? Is she afraid of me? I haven't seen her for two weeks and she's probably heard a lot of angry comments about me during that time.

Ralph opens a bottle of wine and Jaleela pulls a tightly-rolled joint out of her handbag. "Randy brought this back from Colombia," she says handing it to me. "It's for you." Randy's my favorite of her many boyfriends. He's a shy redhead who always carries an old leather doctor's bag full of carefully wrapped samples of hashish, Thai stick, and other delicacies. An Einstein compared to most of her other dealer/lovers, he seems to appreciate Jaleela's intelligence as well as her body. We smoke and drink and eat hamburgers and ice cream. Élan eventually comes over and snuggles into my lap. The others go off to the other room. I imagine them having a threesome. I fall asleep holding Élan. She's the only person in the world I feel safe with.

The next morning Jaleela is hyper. "I need to get back to Fairfax," she says to Ralph. "If you drive me over to the highway, I can hitch back." She reaches into her handbag. "And this is for you guys, for today." She hands Ralph three tabs of acid. He takes them, hands one to Laura and offers me the other.

I shake my head. "No, I'm too screwed up to do acid right now."

"It's really mellow," she says. I shake my head.

Ralph and I drive her a few miles down the road to a good hitch-hiking junction. As she gets out of the truck she holds out the acid again. "Come on, Greg, it's probably just what you need to get you out of your bad mood."

I see a huge wave building up in front of me. Maybe I should just dive into it. "Okay, but I don't want a full hit, just enough to push me through this." I touch the tab of acid with my finger tip, rub it like a genie's lamp, then lick my finger.

"You're not going to get anything from that," she says.

"That's okay," I say. "I don't need it anyway." We hug and she saunters down the road, her outstretched thumb seductively keeping time with her swaying hips. Ralph and I drive back past Sonoma County Mental Hospital. Several patients are sitting by the fence, waving to passing cars. I wave back. Then I start feeling very strange, like my mind is turning inside out.

Ralph looks over. "Are you okay?"

I shake my head. "Man, can you handle a really heavy trip?"

"Sure," he says. Then he looks at me again, less sure. "At least I think so."

## ARREST

Back at the house, Ralph and Laura are both tripping and I'm feeling stranger, more out of control. I lie down on the floor. I'm dying. I'm Marshall Dillon and I've been shot and I'm dying. Kitty is next to me and I lay my head on her lap and tell her I love her. Kitty is Laura and Laura is Kitty. I reach up and caress her breast and she strokes my head.

I feel Élan slide my wallet out of my back pocket. She squats next to me and starts pulling cards out of their plastic covers, scattering them on the floor. I look back at Kitty wanting her to say she loves me. She says nothing. I'm dying unloved in her arms.

Everything from my wallet is scattered around me, my whole life in disarray on the floor. I roll off Kitty's lap onto my knees. This is not right. I have to get my life together. I begin scraping the cards into a pile, trying to sort them out. They won't sort right. Everything is out of control.

I look over at Ralph and Laura. Their faces are distorted. Degenerate carnies trying to woo me into their world of illusion and depravity. I can't stay here. I have to escape from this sham. I have to rescue Élan. I pick her up and head outside. We will walk away, we will breathe fresh air, find a way out of this twisted carnival. Élan is small and wiry, easy to carry. She clings to me like a small monkey, sinuously scrambling up and around my neck and shoulders.

I'm heading somewhere, but I keep forgetting where. My mother's house maybe, or Hanna Boys Center, where my friend Jim Pulskamp is the director. Some place safe. The midday sun burns my shoulders. I sit down next to the road, put Élan down. The hot ground burns her feet. She dances around and scrambles back up on my shoulders. Cars drive by filled with stupid people. I walk out into the road and put up my hand. "Hey!" I yell at a driver, "This is a carnival, man, a sham! You need to get out!" They don't get it. They're robots, blind robots.

I stumble back over to the side of the road. Now I'm afraid. Something is wrong with me. I need help. I need to get back home, to my mother, or to Jim Pulskamp. Everything around me is grey and brown, drab and ugly. Bridget is gone. I am empty, dying.

Élan twists around, repositioning herself on my left shoulder. I look at her, see the sun glistening in her hair. She's beautiful. She and the sunshine are beautiful. The rest of the world is horrible, but she and the sun are beautiful. And she is right here with me. Suddenly it hits me: Why am I grieving the loss of Bridget when here in my arms is the person I really love, my soul mate from many lifetimes? The greys and browns gradually morph into rich, vivid colors. I am the one who has the power to create this world, drab or beautiful. I draw a deep breath into my lungs, feel strength flowing into sagging muscles. I begin to walk with power and purpose, feeling suddenly like a burly Paul Bunyan crashing through a virgin forest. Élan, climbs higher, gripping my neck and ears. I run up an incline beside the road. Her arm slides over my eyes. I can't see. I bump into a steel utility pole, bounce off it back down to the road. A siren sounds in the distance. Bunyan-like, I stride toward it. I smile at Élan. The siren gets louder and a flashing red light comes fast down the road. Good, here's help. Then I catch myself, maybe not. The car skids to a stop across the road. Two beefy cops jump out and run toward me. The first cop has his right hand on his gun. His left is extended in a halt position. "Stop right there. What do you think you're doing?"

"I'm walking."

"No you're not. You're stopping traffic and harassing people."

"I'm just telling them what's happening. That it's all screwed up."

"You're the one who's screwed up, Bud." The cop's stomach bulges over his belt. He squares off in front of me. Something about his attitude reminds me of Ringer when he used to talk about going to work for the World Bank.

"Don't you see?" I tell him. "You don't have to sell out. You can be free of this whole rotten system."

He glares at me under bushy blond eyebrows, moves closer toward me .

Wham! A shoulder smashes into my ribcage. Élan is

ripped out of my arms. She's screaming *Daddy!* hands outstretched as the other cop hustles her away toward the police car. I turn back to the first cop, wading in now, about to grab me. His face is flushed, his eyes beady. I hear a little voice inside me: "This guy is evil, he has to be destroyed." A ball of energy forms in my ankle, moves up my side, rushes through my shoulder and arm into my cocked fist, smashing into his face. Suddenly I'm in grammar school again, rolling on the ground, punching and kicking, spit and blood flying. I taste dirt and feel a knee in my back. My hands are pinned behind me, I'm shoved into the back seat of a car. Doors slam and the car lurches forward. These handcuffs can't hold me, neither can this car. I kick the backseat window hard with my boots, my head and shoulder braced against the opposite door. The cuffs dig into my wrists as I strain to pop the chains. "Don't give up, Élan," I shout through the grate to Élan's curly head up front, "Don't give up! Keep fighting those fuckers!"

The car swerves, then jerks to a sudden stop. I'm about to launch another kick, when the door is yanked open. My head flies out and I look up at a ruddy face glaring down, cigar butt clenched between bared teeth. An arm rearing back. A fist hurtling down.

## HEAVY BEEFS

A sudden shift and the intense pain fades away. I slide through a narrow portal and burst into warm, golden sunlight. Strains of Gregorian chant echo softly. Familiar faces greet me. Mary, the Blessed Mother, kisses my cheek. "Congratulations, my dear, you have passed through death to life." My childhood heroes, St. Tarsisius and St. Lawrence, give me high-fives and wink. This is home, the one I never thought I would find again, the magical place I have missed since childhood. I look back, to that other dark place, and see the soldiers still crowded around my inert body.

Then I am in a perfectly symmetrical cube of four walls. Overhead the sun shines down into a hole that reaches to the molten core of the earth. Centering myself under the glowing sun, I sit in the lotus position over the hole. When I extend my arms, the energy pours into my crown chakra and flows down my spine, resonating love and joy throughout my body. I have become one with Being Itself. This is Heaven.

A sound distracts me momentarily and I reach down to shift my position. The floor feels soft and spongy. I crawl over and feel one of the walls. It feels spongy, too. The golden hue begins to fade and I notice the dull grey of the walls and floor. Everything is changing. I begin to detect an unpleasant odor and look more closely at the hole in the center of the floor. Dried shit is caked around the mouth of it and stale urine sticks to its metal flashing. I look up at the sun, the recent source of my ecstasy. It's actually a bare light bulb. I scan the small room with fresh eyes. It is totally empty, except for some underpants crumpled in one corner. I look down. I am naked. Bruises cover my legs and arms. I hear voices in the hall. A face appears at the small window in the door. "Look at that fucker, man." Derisive laughter. The footsteps retreat. When I push myself up, I feel a sharp pain in my groin. My balls are the size of oranges, delicate to the touch.

Slowly my mind catches up to my senses. I'm not in Heaven. I push the soft wall again. I'm in a padded cell! Fuck! I kick the wall hard with the heel of my foot. How could this happen? Vague memories of Ralph, Laura, the police. Everything is a blur. I kick the wall again. I'm a college professor, for God's sake! I'm a father. An ex-seminarian. Dark, nausea and the familiar feeling of hopelessness envelop me again. Élan. Where is she? Pulling my underwear over my throbbing balls I go to the door and bang on the small window. "Hey!!" The hall is empty, but I can hear voices. I bang louder on the door. "Hey!"

A uniformed guard puts his face to the window. "What?"

"I need to get out of here, I need to find out what

happened to my daughter."

He stares at me. "What were you on?"

"What? Oh. I took a little acid."

"Are you down?"

"Yeah. Yeah, I'm down."

"I'll be back in a few minutes." He walks off.

I pace back and forth, periodically kicking the wall. I think of my mother warning me about drugs. I imagine Bridget being interrupted from some tryst with the news of my fuck-up. Mostly, though, I think of Élan, trying to remember what happened, praying she's okay.

It's at least an hour before the guard comes back. I hear the jingle of keys and rush to the door. He looks in at me warily. "You sure you're down? We don't want to have to fight you again."

"Yeah," I say. "I'm definitely down. Just let me out of here." He unlocks the door and leads me down the hall to a desk. A guy hands me my clothes. My tie-dye T-shirt and jeans are splotched with dried blood and my boots are scuffed. "Get dressed," he says, and sign this. There's a worn manila envelope with lots of crossed-out names. Inside are my belt, wallet, and house keys. I sign on an empty line and hand it back to him.

"You got a lot of heavy beefs on you, buddy." He's looking down at his clipboard.

I'm lacing my boots. "Beefs?"

"Three felony counts. Two for assaulting a police officer, one attempted murder."

"Attempted murder! Who did I attempt to murder?"

"Your little girl's in the hospital in serious condition. You beat her up really bad."

My head swirls. Ideas and images grapple and tumble. That's impossible, I want to say.

"You get one phone call," the guard says and nods toward a wall phone. I ask him for the Sonoma County phonebook and dial Dennis' number. Laura answers on the second ring. "Greg! Where are you?"

"I'm in jail!"

"For what?"

"Attempted murder."

"What??"

"They're saying Élan's in the hospital in serious condition."

"Oh Jesus! Let me talk to them." I hand the phone to the jailor. He tells her the same thing he told me, then says, "Yes ma'am, once he's booked he'll be on the second floor, I'm not sure what cell." He pauses and listens. "I don't know ma'am. That'll be up to the judge." He hands the phone back to me.

Laura's voice is shaky. "Greg, do you remember what happened?"

"All I remember is walking down a road and then punching it out with some cops after they grabbed Élan away from me."

"Okay, don't worry. I'll contact Bridget and we'll find a lawyer. We won't know what the bail is until you see the judge."

"Thanks, Laura. And can you check on Élan, make sure

she's okay?"

I hand the phone back to the jailor. He doesn't look as mean now that he's talked to Laura. "Are the two cops okay?" I ask him, "the ones I fought with?"

"Yeah, they're okay. One of them's pretty pissed though. He ripped a brand new pair of pants fighting with you."

"Tell him I'm sorry, okay?"

He gives me a strange look and laughs. "Yeah, sure."

He leads me down a flight of steps, through a locked door, to a large holding cell. It's all concrete except for the bars around it and the metal toilet in one corner. A dozen men sit on shiny concrete benches. Most stare dejectedly at the floor, ignoring two loudmouth drunks. "That bitch, she's lucky I didn't kill her."

"Got that right," his toothless buddy says, "but lucky for you, you didn't."

"Next time I will though."

"Make sure you fuck her first." They laugh and look around for a response. There is none. I sit on the hard concrete and stare at the floor.

## THE CRUCIFIXION

The drunks have passed out and are snoring loudly by the time a uniformed guard calls my name and escorts me from the holding tank to the booking desk. Another guard rolls my fingers in ink and hands me some bedding and a thin mattress roll. I follow him into an elevator to the next floor. Two jailors meet us and walk me down a long hall. Strange, each step seems to be bringing me closer to a fateful event, something negotiated a long time ago and buried in my unconscious. On either side of the corridor, mysterious figures lurk behind the bars. The jailor unlocks a cell door and points me to a section of bunks on the left. "That empty one's yours."

The common area of the cell is a combination dining room/bathroom. Three guys are sitting on a steel bench watching a snowy version of MASH on a black and white TV mounted on the back wall. Others are sprawled out on their bunks on either side of the main room. Most wear T-shirts and jeans, though an older Hispanic guy is wearing a regular short-sleeved shirt. Everything is stainless steel: tables and benches, freestanding toilets, showerheads, mirror. The Hispanic guy sits on his bunk with his hands folded, looking down at the floor. I ease my bruised balls down on the hard bunk next to his and lay my head back on the coarse blanket.

"Hey man, my name's Hatchet." It's as much a threat as an introduction. "Yours?

I open my eyes. A guy is standing next to my bunk, chewing gum and grinning. His dark hair is combed back into a duck's ass and the sleeves of his white T-shirt are rolled up to show a tattooed bicep.

I push myself up to a sitting position. "Greg, my name's Greg."

He bends over and whispers, "Whatcha in for, Greg?"

I try to look tougher than I feel. "I punched it out with a couple of cops."

He squats down so he's eye level with me. "Okay, here's how it works." He glances over his shoulder and lowers his voice. "Every night we hold court between eight and ten. That's when the guards aren't around. We'll be starting in half an hour. Just wanted to give you a heads-up." He gives me a friendly slap on the arm and walks back to the common area.

I close my eyes and sink back into my private hell, imagining Élan wrapped in bandages, tubes pumping fluids into her body. How could I do something like that? I couldn't. It's impossible. But I can't remember. And if I can't remember how can I be sure? The mental tape-loop rolls on in a nauseating cycle.

"All right, this court will now come to order!" I open my eyes and see Hatchet standing about ten feet away.

Most of the other guys are standing around him in a loose circle. Three of us are still in our bunks – me, the Hispanic guy, and a young kid with longish hair.

"First let's hear from the prosecution," says Hatchet. A big, pockmarked guy steps forward. He points down at the kid in the bunk.

"This fucker, I asked him to pass the salt at dinner and the fucker never passed it. By the time I went to get it, the fucking guard had taken it. I want to fight the fucker."

The kid blinks. He doesn't have a clue. Hatchet looks at him. "Stand up, motherfucker!" The kid gets up from his bunk. His eyes glance around the circle. "So?" Hatchet says. "Let's hear from the defense."

The kid shakes his head. "Man, this is crazy. I didn't hear him ask for the salt. I would have passed it to him."

Hatchet holds up his right hand. "This court rules," he points to the big guy, "they should fight it out."

The group moves in, hungry. The big guy has his fists up, ready.

"No," says the kid. "This is stupid." He drops his hands to his sides. "I'm not going to fight you."

The big guy waves his fists. "Come on, you chickenshit!"

The kid doesn't move, keeps his hands down.

The big guy holds back, waiting.

Bam! Someone else punches the kid from the blind side. "Ow!" yells the kid. "You asshole!" He grabs his jaw, then looks down at his hand for blood. He scans the group again. "Guard!" he yells and moves toward the front bars. "Help! Guard!"

The other prisoners scatter and try to look cool while the kid grips the bars and yells "Guard!" into the empty hall. He keeps yelling. Nobody comes. Gradually his voice gets shakier. "Guard?"

They're off their bunks now, surrounding him again. Hatchet gives him a hard shove. "You motherfucker! You never call the man! You understand? You ever call the man again, we'll kill you. If we don't kill you, we got guys on the outside that'll kill you!"

I'm sitting on the edge of my bunk now, wondering what comes next.

The kid's bent over, cowering. He puts his hands out in front of his chest. "Okay, okay, I understand." Just then a short wiry guy with a shaved head lets out a yell and jumps forward, peppering the kid with punches. He's so manic everybody takes a step back. The kid doesn't yell for the guards this time, he just curls up and takes it. The guy finishes his punching frenzy and dances back into the circle like Mohammed Ali. The guy who didn't get his salt steps in and hits the kid in the face a couple of times. The kid shields his head, waits for more. When none comes he looks out between his hands. "You through?" he says, still just a little cocky.

"No motherfucker." Bam! Bam!

I'm standing now, remembering what I read in Soul on Ice. "Hey brothers, that's not cool. Can't you see what's happening? We're being set up. We should be fighting the guards, not each other."

They all turn around and look at me in my tie-dye shirt

and beard. No one says anything. Hatchet calls court back to order.

The next morning I force my eyes open, hoping to find it was all a bad dream. It is a bad dream and I'm still in it. I sit at the stainless steel table, drink lukewarm watery coffee out of a tin cup, eat powdered eggs and soggy white toast off a tin plate. A guard comes in and reads off names, mine included. "You'll all be called to court around nine o'clock."

The morning snails along. Others are called, I'm not. I sit on my bunk, watching the other prisoners. Hatchet and several others use the stainless steel mirror a lot, combing their hair and adjusting the roll of their sleeves. Others slump near the TV, half-heartedly watching the daytime soaps. I only see one person reading a book, the guy with the shaved head who went berserk last night. He's lying on his bunk and everyone seems to be giving him a wide berth. After a while I walk over there. "Hey man, do they have a library here?"

He looks up at me. "No, just that stack of shit over there." He points to a pile of old paperbacks and magazines near the TV. He comes up on one elbow and marks his place with a finger. "Your first time in the joint?"

"Yeah."

He nods and looks over at the other prisoners. "Well, my advice is don't give these assholes any information about why you're here. You can't trust anybody in jail."

"Thanks for the warning." Damn, why did I blab to Hatchet last night?

After lunch I doze in my bunk. Disjointed images tumble through my mind. I roll over and feel a stab of pain in my testicles. Vague memories of soldiers torturing me. I'm resisting, mocking them for being establishment stooges. They intensify the torture, crucifying me now, nailing first my hands, then my feet. I still refuse to submit to them. They're coming down on me with a drill press, crushing my balls. "No, not even that," I yell, but the pain envelops me in darkness until I am whisked through the last remaining pinhole of light, into that golden home space.

My eyes snap open when I hear a guard call my name. He leads me down the hall to a small room where I see a pudgy guy in a blue suit sitting behind a table, beads of sweat around his temples, smaller ones on his upper lip. His tie knot begs to be loosened. He doesn't stand up when I come in, just nods his head toward the chair opposite him and glances at some papers on the table in front of him. "I wanted to introduce myself," he says. "I'm Alvin Brinker. Your wife has retained me as your lawyer." He looks back at his papers.

"Wasn't I supposed to go to court this morning?" I ask.

"Uh, no. There were some delays. Probably tomorrow." He picks up the papers, shuffles through them, and puts them back in his briefcase. "Do you have any other questions?"

"Yeah. What's happening with my daughter? Is she okay?"

"Oh yeah," he says. "I forgot. Your wife said to tell you

she was in satisfactory condition."

"Satisfactory? What does that mean?"

"I have no details. She just said your daughter was okay." He snaps his briefcase. "So, I'll see you tomorrow." He signals to the guard, and I'm roughly escorted out the door. I walk down the hall feeling like a leper. What a prick!

The afternoon drags on like a redneck soap opera. Hatchet has opinions on everything – cars, women, whiskey, cops – and manages to start stupid arguments with everyone in the cell. I stay in my bunk and try to sleep, but all I can do is replay the bizarre cinema of the past 48 hours. Dinner is awful, lukewarm peas and mashed potatoes with some kind of grey-green meat. I make sure everybody at the table gets plenty of salt. After dinner most of the guys gather around the TV and start arguing about what channel to watch. Some like me go back to their bunks. The guy on the bunk across from me looks as sad as I do, so I start talking to him. "My wife left me right after I got back from 'Nam," he says, "and I got so upset I went out and robbed a music store. Stupid!"

"Hey man, love can do weird things to your head," I say. "Don't be too hard on yourself."

"Yeah," he sniffs. "Still."

Hatchet swaggers in and interrupts us. "Anybody here by the name of McAllister?"

I look up. "Yeah."

"Oh," he says and goes back in the other room. I feel a momentary spark of adrenalin, but it's quickly snuffed by worries about Élan. I roll over on my bunk and bury my head in the pillow. What happened on that road? Did someone hurt her? A few minutes later my introspection is interrupted by Hatchet again, but this time he isn't talking to me. He's over at the far end of the room, next to the wall that separates our cell from the adjoining one. "Hey," he yells around the corner. "Did you guys read tonight's paper?" He has a newspaper in his hand.

"No," says a voice from the next cell.

"Well read this article here," he says, reaching the paper around the bars to the other cell. Maybe thirty seconds go by and then a voice says, "Man, is that fucker in your cell?"

"Yeah, but we're gonna hold court on him tonight," says Hatchet.

"Okay," the voice says. "Let us know and we'll make noise. Be sure and kick him in the balls for us." Hatchet takes the newspaper and goes back to the other room. I think for a minute he might be talking about me but dismiss it. Punching out cops certainly wouldn't be a crime in Hatchet's court. I doze off again, welcoming oblivion.

From a murky dream I hear muffled voices. Turning slightly on my pillow, I half open my eyes. Several pair of feet surround my bunk. I look up into Hatchet's face. "What's your first name?" he says brandishing the newspaper.

"Greg."

He frowns and looks back at the newspaper. "Oh, yeah. Joseph G." He hands me the paper. "Is this about you?" The feeling of impending fate returns. Did I choreograph this in a former lifetime? At least the boredom will soon be over. There's relief in that. The headline reads *Parents Endanger Children's Lives Through Drug Abuse*. I scan down the first three paragraphs, about a woman passing out from sleeping pills, her children throwing cookies on the stove, the house catching fire. I shrug my shoulders at Hatchet. "Keep reading," he says. "Further down."

Oh God. *Mr. Joseph G. McAllister was observed on Arnold Drive carrying his daughter and stopping motorists.* Other details follow: *Acting strangely … disturbing the peace … police called.* Then I see the line that caught Hatchet's attention: *Witnesses say that McAllister was beating his daughter's head against a telephone pole.*

My stomach tightens and tears come to my eyes. Two pairs of rough hands pull me to my feet. "Did you do that?" Hatchet demands.

I look into his eyes and shake my head. "No, Man. I didn't do that."

A punch jolts me to one side. Another. The salt plaintiff is in front of me now, fist cocked. "You fucker! I've got kids of my own!" Knuckles crack against my cheekbone. A knee in my swollen balls doubles me over. I'm on the floor now, rolling into the non-violent defense position I learned in Mississippi. I pull my knees up, lock my arms around my head. Kicks crash in from all sides. Again it feels preordained, almost familiar. I need to follow the script. Don't call for help, but yell "Ow!" loudly enough that the guards will hear you if they're there. They kick my sides and my stomach and propel me out into the common room.

I roll under a table and get a brief respite from the boots. But I'm pulled out again and the kicking continues. Boots thump my back, my legs, the unprotected parts of my head. The floor is getting sticky from my blood. Hatchet calls a halt to the attack. "You're making a mess," he says, pulling me to my feet. "Take a shower." The hard spray stings my eyes, nose, ears, and lips. I watch my blood wash down the open floor drain. When I'm pulled out again, I slip on the wet floor. Their boots crash into my body again. I yell, but I know it's useless. More blood, another shower, a new round of kicks, rolling, slipping, now bent over, kneeling. Thud! A boot hits me in the exposed ribs and I feel a whoosh of air escape. Blood bubbles in my mouth. A punctured lung. I feel my body relax. Everything goes into slow motion. I don't shield my head anymore. Someone kicks my left leg and I hear the bone shudder, but without pain, without any resistance from me. Slowly turning, my head strikes something metal, bounces slightly, hits the floor. I'm in my body yet separate from it, watching. From far away, I hear Hatchet's voice and see his blurry form hovering over me. "Get in your bunk, motherfucker. We'll finish you off after lights-out."

Slowly, I crawl to my bunk and roll onto the rough blanket. Hatchet's standing next to me, surrounded by the others. "Pull down your pants, motherfucker. I'm gonna ass-fuck you."

It feels like a line from a movie script and I hear ambiguity in his voice. I sense his need to create fear in me, but I don't feel fear. I don't feel anything. I roll onto my stomach, unsnap my soggy jeans, and work them slowly down over bruised buttocks. I lie motionless and wait.

Hatchet stands there, then clears his throat. "Well, too bad Smitty ain't still here. He would'a gotten it up." A few snickers and they all walk back into the common room. I keep up the moaning, just loud enough for a guard to hear if he's out in the hall. I also keep spitting up blood. If these guys are planning to finish me off, what do I have to lose?

Hatchet comes every few minutes. He pulls the blanket over my face so no one will see the blood. As soon as he leaves, I pull it down again, spit up more blood, and let out another groan. He paces back and forth the next time he comes in. "If we call the guard, Motherfucker, you better not tell him what happened."

He's gotta be kidding. This whole thing was set up by the guards. No way I'm going to blame the inmates. "What if I tell him I fell in the shower?"

"Okay," Hatchet says, and moments later I hear him yelling through the bars. "Guard! Guard! We need a medic down here in B-1."

It seems like a long time before I hear keys jangling and the cell door opening. A gruff voice says, "Somebody call for a medic?"

Lots of mumbled don't knows. Hatchet yells, "Hey! Anybody call the medic?"

"Not me."

"No, I didn't hear nobody call the medic."

The gruff voice says, "C'mon, you assholes, one of you called the medic."

Hatchet says, "Geez, I don't know. Any of you guys know who called the medic?"

"No, man. We don't know."

"Well fuck it then," the voice says. "I've got better things to do than play games with you guys." The keys jingle again.

"Oh," somebody says, "I wonder if it's that guy over in the back bunk. He didn't look so good earlier. Maybe he called the medic." I hear footsteps approaching my bed. "Yeah, that's him." The guard comes in holding a first aid kit, nervously eyeing the prisoners crowded around him. More blood oozes out of my mouth. He looks down at me. "What's the matter with you, bud?"

I gurgle my prepared response. "I fell in the shower."

"Oh. Stand up."

"I'm not sure I ..."

"I said stand up, motherfucker!" He yanks me to my feet.

I last about three seconds before my knees buckle, and I collapse in a heap. When I come to, I'm in a wheelchair. Someone is rolling me down the hall. We're passing another cell, the one next to us. Prisoners are staring at me from behind the bars, probably the same guys who saw the newspaper. I bet they're thinking Hatchet did a good job.

We go down an elevator and medics transfer me to a gurney, lift me into an ambulance. Bright lights and sirens. One of the medics says, "Geez! What happened to you?"

I'm determined to keep my promise. "I fell in the

shower."

The door opens. They roll me down a corridor under bright lights. We come to a stop. A woman in white leans over me. "Oh my, what happened to you?"

"I fell in the shower."

"Oh come on," she says. "You got beaten up in jail didn't you?'

"No. I fell in the shower." No way I'm going to blame the prisoners for something the guards set up.

A door opens and we roll into a room. People are moving around, arranging things on counters. There are machines with meters and buttons on them. A bright light comes on right over me. Lots of people are standing around me now. An older man with glasses leans in and looks at me. "Wow," he says. "What happened to you?"

I'm feeling groggy, but I say it one more time. "I fell in the shower."

"Man!" The voice over in the corner has a Mississippi twang. "You gotta stay away from that showah!"

I smile. Good line.

## ACHIEVING THE BOTTOM

I float down and re-enter my body. Slowly opening my eyes I see white sheets, tubes hanging down. I flex my jaw and feel bruised bones and a muted pain along my temples. My right hand aches. There's a needle taped to the back of it, feeding fluid from a plastic bag above. Another tube sticks out of my chest and runs into some sort of machine. It, too, is taped securely.

"Hey, you're awake. Feeling better?" The voice is raspy, unfamiliar. I glance right and see what looks like a police uniform.

"Where am I?"

"The Intensive Care Unit of Sonoma County Hospital," he says. "You got beat up in jail night before last."

"What are you doing here?"

"The sheriff has you on round-the-clock surveillance." He puts down the magazine he was reading.

"Why?"

"Not sure. That's just his orders. Three of us pulling eight hour shifts."

"Hmm." I float back inside.

"Mr. McAllister?"

I open my eyes and see a dark figure standing next to me. He's holding something in front of my face. "Mr. McAllister, I'm detective McHenry, Sonoma County Sheriff's Department." It's a badge. "We're anxious to prosecute those inmates who beat you up. If you can just give me their names, or even a description, we'll make sure they get what's coming to them."

My left eye doesn't open all the way when I try to look up at him. All I can make out is a crew cut and a square head. "You're blaming the wrong people," I mumble through a mouth that isn't working any better than my eye. "It's not the prisoners' fault. It's the guards'." I can see him more clearly now, sun-burnished face, dark stubble pushing through weathered pockmarks under hard cheekbones. "The guards take off every night so the prisoners can hold court. It's a setup."

"Well, we can look into that," he says, "but we have to start with the prisoners who did the actual beating. Can you remember any of their names?" He pulls out a small notebook.

"If I go after anybody it'll be the guards."

He closes his notebook and sets his jaw. "You're making a big mistake. Without your cooperation, we can't do anything to stop this."

"How about starting with the guards?"

He fishes a card out of his jacket pocket and slaps it down on the bed tray. "Think about it. If you change your mind, give me a call." He looks over at the sheriff's deputy, shakes his head, and walks out of the room.

That afternoon I wake up to Bridget standing next to my bed. She's wearing a shear paisley dress that highlights her newly slimmed figure. There are tears in her eyes as she looks down at me. She sits on the bed and gently kisses the stitches on my mouth. "Élan's at my mom's house," she says. "She's fine."

"Really? That lawyer told me she was in *satisfactory* condition. I figured she was still in the hospital."

"That jerk! I told him to tell you they released her. She's fine, not a scratch on her. I'm going to fire him and get a new lawyer."

"God, that's a relief! I was so worried about her."

Bridget strokes my cheek. "I know. But don't worry. Everything's going to be fine. We're all going to be just fine." She rests her head against my shoulder. I smell the shampoo on her hair, feel her softness against my bruises. I hope she's right.

Later that afternoon, my mother tiptoes into my room. When she sees me she lets out a wimper. "Look at you!"

"Don't worry, Ma. It's not as bad as it looks."

She sinks down on the bed, searching my face with frightened, puffy eyes.

"I screwed up," I say, smiling through my stitches.

"I just thank God you're alive," she whispers, wiping away a tear.

A week later, I sit on the deputy's chair, waiting for him to come back with a wheelchair. It feels strange wearing regular clothes after two weeks of hospital gowns.

"Okay, the van's downstairs," he says, rolling the chair in

and locking the brake. "Time to go see the judge."

Bridget is waiting with our new lawyer outside the small courthouse in Sonoma. With his long beard and crumpled black suit, he could be mistaken for a Hassidic rabbi if it wasn't for his paisley tie. "Okay," he says, rubbing his hands together, "this should go fast. The judge has the reference letters. Our goal today is to get you out on your own recognizance. We'll worry about the trial later."

Bridget has obtained letters of support from Sister Patch, the president of Lone Mountain College where I teach, Jim Pulskamp, the director of Hanna Boys Center, and several other community people. The judge, Edwin McMahon, is old and conservative, reputed to be very tough on drugs, which makes me nervous. I sit between Bridget and my mother and watch McMahon page though the documents on his desk. Finally he looks up and nods to my lawyer. "Your honor," my lawyer says, "in light of the sheriff's apparent inability to protect his prisoners from assault, and in light of my client being an upstanding citizen and having no prior record of any kind, we would ask the court to release Mr. McAllister on his own recognizance."

The judge glares at him, then looks back at the letters on his desk, seemingly confused by this unlikely coalition of priests, nuns and Jewish lawyers. He keeps looking down at his desk while he talks. "Having reviewed these letters, I have no choice but to release the defendant on his own recognizance, pending criminal trial." Bridget gives my hand a squeeze. "However," the judge says, squinting over steel-rimmed glasses, "I cannot in good conscience allow this defendant to have any physical contact with his daughter. Is there a relative with whom she can stay when Mr. McAllister returns home?"

Bridget's parents are both on their feet volunteering – a little too hastily, it seems to me. My lawyer stands up to object, but the judge cuts him off. "I hereby release the defendant on his own recognizance with the stipulation that he is absolutely forbidden to have any physical contact with his daughter. Is that clear?" Bridget's folks are nodding obsequiously. Other people in the courtroom are eyeing me warily, like I'm some kind of monster.

Back at the hospital, my room feels empty. The machines and drip scaffolds have been removed, no nurses come to check my temperature. Tomorrow morning Bridget will come and take me home. Except that I have no home. Not really, not without Élan. I look at the empty chair next to my bed. Funny, I miss the deputy. He gave me some vestige of self-worth that's gone now. I look out the window at the trees and rooftops spread out below. Five years ago I was a deacon, preaching sermons to the people in those houses, visiting this same hospital in my Roman collar. That's when I made my deal with God. "This is too easy," I said to Him, "this fancy rectory, three meals a day, a free car, people twice my age calling me *Father*. I feel like I'm on top of the heap without having paid my dues. Let me experience the bottom. Then maybe I'll be ready to be a priest."

PART THREE:

# THE GLORIOUS MYSTERIES

# DÉJÀ VU

"It'll never stand. We're going to appeal it." My lawyer is at his desk, tie loosened, sleeves rolled up on hairy forearms. Circles of sweat darken the armpits of his blue shirt. "The hospital checked her. She had no injuries. That judge never read the medical report, just the newspaper account. What a prick!"

"But in the meantime, I still can't see her," I say. "How long is this going to take?"

"If we lose the appeal, we'll waive the preliminary hearing. That'll speed up the trial date. In the meantime, line up some character witnesses for yourself."

Almost every night I talk to Élan on the phone. "Grandma and I went shopping today," she reports, "and I played on Grandpa's tractor." Bridget reports that she seems to be doing fine, doesn't seem upset. I'm the one who needs reassurance. "You'll be home soon, Sweetie," I keep telling her. "I promise."

The court appoints a psychiatrist to examine me. I meet him at his office in the back of his house in San Anselmo. He peers at me over bottle glasses. "You appear to have suffered a temporary psychosis," he says, "caused by stress, but precipitated by the LSD." He's a mousy little guy. I'm not sure I trust him or his diagnosis. But then he takes off his glasses and leans back in his chair, massaging the grooves in the bridge of his nose. "You know, Greg, you're living totally in your head. You've decided which emotions are okay and which ones aren't, and you won't let yourself feel any of the bad ones, like jealousy, anger, fear." He puts his glasses back on and smiles at me. "They're the ones that'll kick your ass if you don't acknowledge them."

My trial date is three weeks later. I walk in with my lawyer and see my mother and her neighbor, Mickey, sitting on a wooden bench outside the courtroom, dressed as though they're going to church.

"Mom, you remember my lawyer, Steve Turer."

She reaches out and takes his hand. Her eyes register his long hair and Picasso tie. "Nice to see you again, Steve." Her smile is tight. She's trying her best to stay detached from this whole thing.

Mickey reaches across and grabs Steve's hand. "I'm a character witness. Will they be cross-examining me?"

Steve sits down next to her. "I'm hoping you won't have to testify at all, but if you do and they ask you questions, just tell them the truth. There's nothing to worry about." He looks at his watch. "I have to make a quick call. I'll be right back."

"Before you go, where's the bathroom?" I ask.

He points over my shoulder. "Down to the right."

My stomach is churning. I need to splash some cold water on my face. Heading down the hall, I open the bathroom door, almost bumping into a burly guy in an ill-fitting suit. "Sorry," I mumble. His eyes momentarily meet mine and get very large just before he ducks around me and scurries down the hall. In the bathroom, I cup my hands under the faucet and pool cold water against my eyes. The image of the man's face suddenly flashes back into focus behind my eyelids. His eyes are mean. A cigar butt is wedged between his clenched teeth.

We enter the courtroom and I sit in the first row behind the lawyers' table. Next to me, my mother sits straight up in her chair, looking down at the purse on her lap. Mickey pats her hand and winks at me. My lawyer whispers to his partner. At the other end of the table a young man in a grey suit arranges papers in front of an empty chair. The engraved nameplate reads *Gary Antolini, Assistant District Attorney.*

Antolini. There was a Gary Antolini in the class ahead of me at St. Anselm's. I can see him walking across the playground in the seventh grade, a thin, dark-haired kid who smiled a lot. Across the courtroom, the guy from the restroom enters through a side door and sits down. He glances over at me but looks away as soon as he sees me looking back. Then a dark suit bustles past me and takes the empty chair at the table. He's about the right age for Antolini, though he's gained weight and his hair is starting to grey. The young assistant starts handing him papers. Antolini quickly scans each sheet then grabs the next one. "I think that DA went to St. Anselm's with me," I whisper to my mother.

She rolls her eyes and shakes her head. "Let's hope he doesn't remember you."

The door behind the judge's bench opens and a bailiff appears. "All rise. Court is now in session, Judge Joseph P. Murphy presiding." My jaw drops. Murphy?? Murphy was the judge I met when I was a deacon, the one who called me naïve when I advocated for that welfare mother. The black-robed figure walks in, and I see his short, grey-flecked hair. It's Murphy, all right. I wonder if he'll recognize me after five years. Probably not, with the beard; but he might remember my name.

## COURTROOM RASHOMON

"Mr. Antolini, call your first witness."

"Prosecution calls Deputy Donald Holzhauser to the stand."

The guy from the restroom walks over to the witness stand, adjusting his tie. My heart beats faster. Antolini starts to question him about the suspect he arrested on Arnold Drive on June 16th. "Do you see the suspect in this courtroom?"

"Yes Sir," he says and points at me. My brain snaps into focus as everyone in the courtroom turns and looks my way. Antolini nods. "Has his appearance changed since you last saw him?"

"Yeah," Holzhauser says, "he's lost quite a bit of weight, I'd say about twenty pounds."

What? Is he crazy? I weigh exactly the same. Did the LSD turn me into some sort of Incredible Hulk? Antolini leans back against the railing. "Could you describe what happened on June 16th?"

Holzhauser clears his throat and tugs at his shirt cuff. "Officer Speridon and I got a call at about 2:15 p.m. concerning an adult male disrupting traffic on Arnold

Drive near Glen Ellen. We approached the scene and observed the defendant standing in the middle of the road holding a child in his arms. He was stopping traffic and shouting." He looks up at Antolini who nods him on. "We approached the subject and attempted to communicate with him, but without success. At that point, we decided our best course of action was to separate the child from the defendant. Officer Speridon went around behind him and grabbed the child while I engaged him from the front. I was about to restrain him, when I was struck on the left cheek by the defendant's clenched right fist. When I attempted to grab him again, I was struck on the right cheek by the defendant's clenched *left* fist."

I glance out the corner of my eye at my mother. She's sitting absolutely still, her hands tightly folded.

"Officer Speridon and I eventually subdued the defendant and transported him and the child to the county jail where we arranged for the child to be taken to the hospital."

Antolini asks a few more questions and then turns him over to my lawyers for cross examination.

Steve Turer walks over to the witness stand. "Officer Holzhauser, did you observe the defendant actually harming his daughter in any way?"

Holzhauser shakes his head. "No, he was just acting weird and intimidating motorists."

"Thank you. No more questions."

The DA's next witness is an old Italian guy in coveralls. He tells Antolini he works for the city and was fixing a water main down the street when the police arrived. "I hear sirens and then I see the police drive up and arrest somebody."

Antolini looks down at his papers. "Did you see anything before that?"

"No, I'm down in the hole. I don't see anything."

"How about the person they arrested, did you see him?"

"No, he's too far away. I can't make him out."

Antolini looks down at his notes and sighs. "No further questions." He walks back to the table and grabs another sheet of paper from his red-faced assistant.

I feel like I'm watching a film of my life told from different points of view, as in Rashomon. My mother is still staring down at her lap. For her, this is a horror movie.

"The prosecution calls Neil Maloney."

An obese man pads over to the witness stand. He's wearing a short-sleeved polyester shirt that slopes across his belly then falls straight down like a tablecloth. His responses are eager and officious. "The guy was obviously high on drugs, Sir. I personally spent two years as a medic in Vietnam, so I know a drug addict when I see one."

Antolini walks closer to the witness stand. "And what was the defendant doing when you first observed him?"

"He was hitting his daughter against a telephone pole."

My mother lets out a gasp. I hold my breath as Antolini asks him to repeat what he just said.

At the cross examination my lawyer walks over to a whiteboard and pastes up a large diagram of the site where I was arrested. "Mr. Maloney, can you show the court exactly where you were standing when you first observed the defendant?" He marks Maloney's location with an X. "And where exactly was the telephone pole?"

Maloney hesitates for a minute then points to a spot up to the right.

The lawyer marks it with an O. "Have I drawn this accurately, Mr. Maloney?"

Maloney studies the diagram. "Yes Sir, I think that's correct."

"No more questions. Thank you, Mr. Maloney."

Maloney looks surprised and glances over at Antolini, who is busy shuffling through his files. After a second, the judge says, "Thank you, Mr. Maloney, you may step down now."

Emil Fritchi is the last witness called. He's a big man with sunburned cheeks and sandy hair. He repeats the oath in a husky Southern voice. Antolini walks over toward him. "How did you happen to witness the arrest on June 16th?"

"I run the wine shop next to where it happened," Fritchi says. "I'm the one who called the police."

Antolini nods, "So you saw the whole thing from start to finish?"

"Yes Sir."

"And what was the defendant doing when you first saw him?"

"Well," Fritchi drawls, "I first seen him standing out in the middle of Arnold Drive, holding his daughter in his left arm and banging on the hood of a lady's white

Cadillac, yelling at her."

"Could you hear what he was yelling?"

"Yessir, I could."

"And can you tell us what you heard?"

Fritchi looks up at the judge, "I don't rightly know as I should repeat it in court."

"Please," says Antolini, "we need it for the record."

"Fritchi looks sheepishly at the judge, "Well, he was calling her a 'mother fucker.'"

My mother groans and Mickey puts her hand on her arm. Fritchi's face is red and he's looking down at the floor. "All right, Mr. Fritchi," says Antolini, "can you tell us what happened then?"

"Then he ran up a little bank beside the road, and there was one of those steel utility poles. He must not have seen it, cause he banged into it and stumbled back down to the road. About that time I heard the sirens and seen the police arrive. They argued with him for a while and then one of them grabbed the little girl away from him. He got real mad and went after the other fella. Took both of them to get him down."

When it's his turn, Steve Turer points to the diagram. "Mr. Fritshi, is this an accurate drawing of the arrest location?"

Fritshi squints at the diagram. "Yeah, I'd say that's pretty good."

"Can you show us where you were standing when you observed the defendant?" Fritshi tells him and he marks an X on the board. "And you had an unobstructed view from there?"

Fritshi nods. "Yessir."

"Now if someone were standing over here," he points to Maloney's X, "would he have a good view of the defendant?"

Fritshi shakes his head. "No, he'd be looking through some trees."

"And the telephone pole, is this about where the telephone pole would be?" Steve points to the O.

Fritchi frowns at the diagram and shakes his head. "There isn't any telephone pole out there. Just one of those little utility poles and that's off to the right."

Steve puts a new O where Fritshi points. "Now when the defendant ran up that incline and collided with the pole, would his daughter have been hit by the pole?"

"No," says Fritchi, "he had his arm around his daughter. Likely the pole would have hit his arm, not the little girl."

Antolini slams his pencil on the table and whispers to his assistant, louder than he probably intends, "Who the Hell got this case together, anyway?"

After the cross examination, the judge calls a recess and beckons the lawyers up to the bench. Mickey leans over and says, "Do you think I'll still get called?" I shrug.

The lawyers are huddled around the judge's bench, nodding. When they finish, Steve walks back to where I'm sitting. He leans in and whispers. "The DA is willing to drop the felony charges if you're willing to plead guilty to disturbing the peace and resisting arrest. Those are both misdemeanors. The judge says if you plead guilty, he'll suspend the sentence and put you on probation. I think it's a good deal."

I nod, "Yeah, especially since that's what I'm actually guilty of. But what about Élan?"

Steve grins. "He just lifted the restraining order."

Outside the courtroom Holzhauser is talking to Antolini. As he turns to go, I touch his arm. "Hey man, I want to apologize for punching you."

He glares at me for a second, then stalks off. He must still be mad about those pants.

## WATERGATE

"Watch out Daddy!"

I lower my head as Élan sails out of the loft on her rope swing and lands on the end of my bed. Our cottage is tiny, just one small room with a narrow kitchen out front and a small bathroom to the side. Its windows look out on a beautiful backyard rose garden behind an old San Francisco mansion. This was the original gardener's cottage. I moved in a year ago, in 1973, after my second, and final, breakup with Bridget. Élan has been with me for several months, ever since Bridget sold the house in Fairfax and went on an extended trip to Europe. Every morning, Élan and I head off to Lone Mountain College together, where she plays in the new, student-run day-care center and I teach my classes in Mass Media and Propaganda. This semester I've been using the Watergate Hearings as a case study, and I've gotten so mesmerized by them that I've decided to resign at the end of the year and move to Washington D.C. where some friends are living in a commune.

It's a bright June morning when Élan and I pack our things into the VW camper. She stuffs the small closet full of clothes, first hers, then her doll's. We say goodbye to the friend who is subletting the cottage, and head into the fog, toward the Bay Bridge. I fiddle with the radio until I find some rock music. Élan pirouettes around the back of the camper for a while, then stretches out on a sleeping bag and starts paging through one of her books. Soon she's asleep. An hour later I see her head pop up. "Daddy, can we find a playground with a jungle gym?" We turn off the freeway and take back roads through several small towns until we spot a park with monkey bars. This becomes our daily afternoon ritual.

The commune is in an old house at 14th and Q, the heart of D.C.'s red-light district. My friends Michael and Karen are living here, along with their daughter Lucy who is Élan's best friend. On warm nights we sit out on the stoop and watch the streetwalkers sashay down the sidewalk. They always stop and talk to Élan and Lucy. "Oh, you so pretty! What's your names?" Washington is not what I expected. No one here seems as concerned about Watergate as I am. For them it's just another political scandal, one among many.

After a long, extremely hot summer, Élan and I decide to head back home by way of New York and Boston. As we drive past the stock exchange on a warm October afternoon and head up Wall Street, hordes of people, many of them wearing yarmulkas, start pouring into the streets. Traffic comes to a halt. "What's going on?" I yell to a young man in a black suit. "Beginning of Rosh Hashanah," he says, glancing down at his watch. "Everybody's trying to get home by sundown." It takes us thirty minutes to get to the next block. I feel trapped. "Élan, let's head for Montana, okay?" She nods and we flounder around downtown until we spot a sign to the Verrazano Bridge. Three days later we arrive at my uncle's house in Lewistown, Montana.

## ON THE ROAD

By the time we get back to San Francisco, Bridget has returned home from Europe. She and Élan rush into each other's arms squealing and laughing. Suddenly I feel superfluous. I return to my cottage, but it feels bare without Élan swinging from her loft. A month later, when Craig suggests we pull up stakes and try our luck in Denver, I don't have to think twice. Élan is happily reunited with Bridget, and there's nothing else holding me in San Francisco.

I'll keep wandering for the next five years. I'll explore the rural towns of Colorado, settle briefly in Telluride as a freelance writer, interview Julie Christi at the first Telluride Film Festival. Then I'll hitchhike to Montana and jump freights through Washington and Oregon. I'll sleep in hobo jungles and learn how broken men pass their days without hope or expectation. I'll set chokers for a beer-drinking-but-born-again logger who curses and shakes his fist at Heaven every time something breaks. I'll work as a security gardener in a dope patch, and then spend a year on a farm with an elderly couple who read books every night and have never seen a TV. I'll help a friend build a pyramid out of driftwood and pine logs, and spend a month with a spiritualist in Seattle who informs me that clouds are really just camouflage for Venetian space ships. I'll deliver honey for a New Age beekeeper whose astrologer predicts my truck will break down in August. It does, and the mechanic tells me it's a problem with the planetary gears. I'll talk to the national president of the John Birch Society and almost convince him that marijuana smokers should have the same rights as gun owners. I'll befriend dreadlocked radicals and bouffanted born-agains, alkies and teetotalers. I'll listen to their stories and fold their dueling conspiracy theories into an ever-expanding narrative that tries to embrace everything and everyone, no matter how crazy. I'll try to fill the hole that's been there since I left the seminary. I'll return to celibacy and imagine myself a Percival in search of the Holy Grail. But when my search is still unfulfilled, I'll lose patience and summon Jesus into one of my dreams. He'll appear before me with his maddeningly beatific smile.

"You bastard!" I say. "All my life you've been calling me to something, and I've followed you down some pretty weird paths. But I'll be damned if I know what you want me to do." He smiles again, so I poke him hard in the chest. "I'm almost fifty years old and I still don't know." He just nods, which pisses me off, so I jab him harder and get right in his face. "All I want is a little clarity, just a little friggin' clarity!"

He stops smiling and puts up his hands, backing me off. Then he turns his head as though he's talking to someone, his Father I assume. He turns back and shrugs. "What can I say?" he says. "We need you under deep cover a little longer."

I wake up laughing, very relieved. I'm okay after all.

## CELESTE

About that time I fall in love again. Hard. Celeste is the most stunning woman I've ever seen, tall and thin with dark curly hair and a flawlessly beautiful face. I watch her glide through the Bombay Club dining room, effortlessly moving from table to table with drinks and entrees. I look forward to the lulls in the dinner rush, when she will come into my service bar for a cigarette. She is an artist, deeply spiritual, and I find her easy to talk to. She has a four-year-old son, a supportive ex-husband, and a spirited boyfriend who often shows up at the end of the night to take her home. While she waits for him, she sits at the bar with the other waiters and kitchen staff, taking advantage of the employee discount on drinks. When I do the books in the morning, I notice that her paycheck is often wiped out by her bar bill.

Eventually she breaks up with the boyfriend, which sends him over the edge for a while. He periodically invades the dining room to badger her with cocaine-fired protestations of love and grief. The gay waiters are frightened of him, so it falls to me to calm him down. I become Celeste's confidante during this time, partly because of my role as manager, but also because of a growing attraction between us.

One night she needs a ride home, so I take her on my motorcycle. She asks if I'd like to come in for a drink.

"Actually," I say, "what I'd really like to do is spend the night with you."

We make gentle love that first night, amazed at how perfectly our bodies seem to fit together, as though they were designed for each other. I am rapturous, convinced that I have finally found my soul mate. She seems to feel the same way, but then gradually pulls away and decides to give her boyfriend another chance. I am devastated. He's certainly more handsome and passionate than me, more like the Clark Gable partner she has fantasized since seeing *Gone With The Wind* as a young girl. I can't compete with that.

I tell her I love her, but that I am willing to let her go if that's what she wants. She says she loves me too, and we both cry. During the next year, she moves in and out of my life several times, then Fate finally intervenes. After an escape to Montana, she calls to tell me she is pregnant.

I welcome the news. "I've been in love with you since I first saw you, and the way I figure, this is the only way you'll stick around long enough for me to prove it."

When Celeste gets back to Denver, we take her four-year-old-son out to dinner and tell him we've decided to get married. When he only responds with a grunt, I prod him a bit:

"Come on. Tell me what you're thinking. Is that okay

or not?"

He looks at me across the table, frowning. "Well, you can marry my mom, but you can't sleep with her."

My daughter has a similar reaction. She has had me to herself for the last four years, and the first time she hears me call Celeste "Sweetie" she jams her finger into her chest and declares, "I'm Sweetie!"

Six months later, our son is born after an eleven-hour labor. Celeste, adamant about natural childbirth, fights her way to that goal, despite the fetal monitor that periodically seems to squeal "C-section, C-section!" to all the attendants on duty. The baby finally pops out with his umbilical cord wrapped around his neck, but as soon as his vocal cords are unwound, he lets out a wail that dispels any fear about him being short of breath or vigor.

We've already agreed to name him "Shane," after Jack Schaefer's famous western hero. I met Mr. Schaefer at a Western film festival in Santa Fe in 1981 and am fascinated by his story. Shane was the first book he ever attempted, he said, writing it late at night to unwind after the stress of meeting a midnight newspaper deadline. He sent his only copy to a publisher and, when he got no response, assumed that the story was unworthy of publication. A year later, he received a letter: *Dear Mr. Schaefer, you are a very lucky man. I never accept unsolicited manuscripts, but somehow yours ended up in a pile on my desk. I just finished reading it and I happen to really like it. You are a very lucky man.*

Schaefer told the film festival audience that, even though he wrote the book, he would not take any credit for the movie, because he had totally opposed casting Alan Ladd as Shane. "Ladd was a short, pretty boy,' he said. "He wasn't the Shane in my book.'

When I re-read the book, sure enough, Shane is described as a tall, wiry, well-groomed gentleman with a rather intimidating and mysterious aura and a relentless sense of honor. That's the Shane we choose to name our son after, not Alan Ladd.

Scarcely a week after he is born, Shane lives up to his name by saving a guy's life in a barroom brawl. Really.

Celeste decided that day to bring Shane to meet her sister Trixie who was bartending in a biker joint called the 4-U on East Colfax. The whole family decides to come with us. It's a hot afternoon, and there are only a few grizzly regulars playing pool in the back room, so Trixie puts Shane up on the bar in his carrier so she can "ooh" and "aah" over him. While we're standing there, the door opens and a big Black guy in a Stetson hat and leather coat – strangely ill-chosen, it occurs to me, for the 90 degree weather outside - comes in and ambles over to the poolroom. Moments later we hear shouting from that direction and one of the regulars comes flying out, bleeding from the forehead, hotly pursued by the Black guy, who now is openly swinging the tire iron he'd concealed up the sleeve of his leather coat. Instead of heading out the door, the bleeding fugitive runs over toward us and cowers down in front of the bar, right below Shane. The Black guy hovers over him, waving his tire iron. I jump between them and push my hands against his chest.

"Man, did you notice there's a baby on the bar right in front of you?"

The guy's eyes move from his squirming victim up to Shane, and his jaw drops.

"God! I'm sorry, man! I never saw him. I was too busy dealing with this sorry-assed motha-fucker down here. I'm really sorry."

He gives his cowering target a few more words of warning and then turns to us, apologizes again, and walks out. Shane is just lying there, like a miniature Buddha. "This kid!" I think, "He not only managed to bring Celeste and me together, but now, barely a week old, he saved some grifter's life."

But even Shane is unable to save our marriage. Celeste gradually slides away from me into the mysterious inner space of her art, and I begin to feel used and unloved. Finally, after nine years, we sadly separate, realizing that we love in different, incompatible ways.

## FAREWELL

The hospital bed is tilted up about 30 degrees, just enough to make swallowing and breathing easier. She's in and out of consciousness now, sucking in air and then lying motionless for long periods. I lean in close and whisper into her ear. "It's okay Mama. We love you. It's okay to let go." My mother is preparing to leave the earth plane. She seems ready. This morning, when her breathing became labored, Sister Antoinette asked, "Are you all right, Ullainee?" My mother smiled up at her through soft, milky eyes. "Yes, Sister, that's the trouble." Sally Pola is standing on the other side of her bed. She was our neighbor in Kentfield, my "older sister" during childhood, and has remained close to my mother ever since. "She's almost gone," she whispers.

I can't imagine life without her. I think back on all we've been through together, her happiness when I entered the seminary, her pain when I left, her terror when I stopped attending church, her anger when I got Bridget pregnant. I remember the grief on her face when she visited me in the hospital after I was beaten in jail. That was thirty years ago, before my hobo phase when I hit the road and wandered through Oregon and Colorado, trading labor for room and board. "I prayed for you during that time," she told me recently, "and entrusted you to the Blessed Mother." Her faith has never flagged, though it eventually evolved beyond dogmatic Catholicism. A few weeks ago I asked her, "Are you looking forward to being reunited with Dad in Heaven?" She smiled and her eyes floated toward the ceiling. "Oh, that would be wonderful! But I have no idea what's going to happen. I just leave that in the hands of God."

I feel Élan's hand, gentle on my shoulder. The bond we forged on that dusty road thirty years ago has grown deeper through the years. She came to live with me in Denver when she was ten, and the two of us were together until she finished high school and headed to New York to study dance with Alvin Ailey. She and my mother are remarkably similar – independent, funny, generous. And they both chose older men. Élan's partner stands in the corner, a crusty New York businessman, hard driving and cynical, not comfortable in emotional situations. When my mother met him four years ago, I was curious about what her verdict would be. "I like him very much," she said. "He's very straightforward and seems to have his head screwed on right." He liked her too. I glance over at him and am surprised to see a tear coursing down his cheek.

Across from me Celeste is holding my mother's hand, her eyes red and puffy. She and I raised a wonderful son, but we have been separated for the last seven years. I see her eyes fixed on my mother's face, radiating her warm, spacious love. If only my heart could have been satisfied with that kind of diffracted love.

My mother rasps another breath and then lies quiet. Will this be her last? Is she hovering above us already? Last week I told her, "I don't know what the rules are once you pass over, Ma, but if it's allowed, will you come back and give me some advice?" She laughed and waved a dismissive hand. "Oh, of course."

No breathing now for some time. Her eyes are almost closed. I glance over at Sally and we exchange sad nods. Élan tightens her grip on my shoulder. A sudden short gasp, a jerk of her shoulder. "It's okay, Mama," I whisper. "You can go now. I love you." Silence.

"She's gone," Sally says. I kiss my mother's thin lips, touch her dry cheekbone.

The funeral is held in the Nazareth Home chapel where my mother attended daily Mass during her three-year residence here. She loved this place, run by the Sisters of Nazareth, Irish nuns dedicated to elder care. Sister Regina, bent over with arthritis, grabs my hand with gnarly fingers. "Greg, we'll miss your mother. She was a real lady." She jerks her head toward the elderly residents standing nearby. "Never a whiner, like most of these."

Pat Browne says the Mass and a group of seminary classmates sing Gregorian Chant. Arnie Kunst plays the organ. Most of them have become, not priests, but teachers, social workers, lawyers, therapists. McLaughlin still doesn't like to sing, but he stands with us and mouths the words. The nuns hear the Latin chant and smile from the back of the chapel. When it's time for the sermon, Pat invites me to the pulpit. I look out at Bridget and her mother, just as I did thirty-five years ago during my first sermon at St. Rose Church. Élan and Celeste are in the front pew. I see elderly teachers who once worked with my mother, her former principal, friends from the old neighborhood. I tell them how she got the name Ullainee; I relate her story about blowing a police whistle into the boys' bathroom and forcing everyone to come out, even the workmen painting the stalls. I thank them all for loving her.

When the reception and burial are over, I slip back into the chapel one last time. Despite my distrust of organized religion, this is still my grounding point. I close my eyes and float into my mother's presence. "Live life, Dear," I hear her say. "It's okay to be happy." I open my eyes and glance over at the statue of the Blessed Mother. Was that a wink?

# EPILOGUE

## DANCING

Nine Years Later . . .

"How'd you two flatlanders end up in Vermont?"

The question has a tinge of challenge, but I don't think Everett Morrow means it that way. He's just trying to make awkward conversation with us newcomers across the table. These community suppers are about the only time he leaves his dairy farm.

"Serendipity," Leah says, and smiles at him.

Everett lifts one eyebrow and cocks his head. "How so?"

"We used to work together in Denver," she says. "We were just friends. Then Greg moved to the East Coast and invited me out for a visit. That's when we got together. We visited a friend in Brattleboro, liked it enough to move there, then we found Putney."

"You left out the best part," I say. Leah looks at me and rolls her eyes. Everett wipes a dab of salad dressing from the corner of his mouth. "And what's that?" he says.

"The magic rocking chair." I wait and watch Everett's weathered face twist into a quizzical grin. "My mom died nine years ago and I kept her favorite rocking chair. When

I decided to leave Denver, it wouldn't fit in my car, so Leah offered to keep it at her house until I settled someplace." Everett nods at me over smudgy glasses. "A few months later she sent me an e-mail. She didn't want me to think she was nuts, she said, but she'd been sitting in the rocker one night and heard my mother talking to her, saying, 'You need to ask Greg to take you dancing.'"

Leah breaks in, "I never met his mother, and I had no idea if he even liked to dance."

Everett leans toward me. "And what did you do?"

I shrug. "Well, it made sense. My mother knew I liked to dance, and she was always better than me at picking marriage partners. So I said yeah, okay, let's dance. And I invited Leah out for a visit."

Everett grins and shakes his head back and forth. "And how long ago was that?"

"Almost seven years," Leah says. "We've been dancing ever since."

"Well." Everett shakes his head again. "Sounds like your mama knew what she was doin'. Welcome to Vermont."

Photo by John Ravnik

## ABOUT THE AUTHOR

Greg McAllister is a former seminarian, playground director, college instructor, truck driver, bartender, radio announcer, restaurant manager, career advisor, newsletter editor, filmmaker, and education benefits manager. After receiving his BA in Philosophy, he studied Theology for three years, then earned an M.A. in CreativeArts Interdisciplinary Studies from San Francisco State University and an MSW from Colorado State University. He has lived and worked in Northern California, Colorado, Oregon, Washington D.C., New York, Connecticut, and Vermont. He currently lives with his wife, Linda, in Vermont where he writes, makes films, and works as a hospice volunteer. He has two grown children, and enjoys traveling by bicycle, snowshoe, motorcycle and kayak.

CPSIA information can be obtained at www.ICGtesting.com
Printed in the USA
BVOW08s1510260415

397752BV00018B/621/P